ULRICH F. ZWYGART

LEADERS

HOW TO
AVOID FAILING

HOW TO
DEVELOP

HOW TO
STAY ON TOP

First published in German with the title
"(Ir-)Rationale Topmanager, Zur Krise der Finanzwirtschaft und des Managements"
Copyright by Verlag Neue Zürcher Zeitung, Zürich 2012
ISBN 978-3-03823-789-3

Cover design: Alexandre Cuennet, www.alexandrecuennet.com
Design, typesetting: Lautes Haus GmbH, Bern
Printing, binding: LuLu.com

ISBN 978-1-291-77964-6

For all managers in Finance

Contents

"Some think that we are made good by nature, others by habituation, others by teaching."

Aristotle

Introduction: The motivation for this book

In 2008 banks dragged the financial markets into a crisis that infected wide swaths of the world economy. Nonetheless, they have since then continued to pay salaries and bonuses that are far above the level seen in other economic sectors, leaving many people appalled and mistrustful. Financial products are being created that customers no longer understand, and top managers are making decisions that are incomprehensible to the public. While countless people were being put out of work and companies were vanishing, banks were benefitting from governmental bailouts, all the while paying colossal severance packages to departing CEOs and astronomical bonuses to their top managers. Banks have suffered an enormous loss of confidence.

The financial and economic crisis is, at the same time, a management crisis: From their specific point of view, managers seem to have believed that they were acting rationally, but when viewed from the perspective of their companies and society as a whole, their actions were irrational. Who is responsible for this generation of managers? Universities certainly, especially business schools, but also global financial institutions, which leave their top managers to their own devices or at any rate do very little to monitor them – as long as the deals they make are profitable. The crisis in modern management can also be attributed to management science, with its dogged emphasis on best practices, *homo oeconomicus*, and specialized expertise. Research and teaching activities have been overwhelmingly dominated by the paradigm which holds that a rational analysis of past economic success is certain to offer patented steps for future action, as well as by the concept that top managers make rational and, therefore, prudent decisions.

This book takes a critical view of *homo oeconomicus*,[1] i.e., the theory that humans are rational actors, because it is unrealistic and misleading: Top managers do not consistently act in a rational manner with respect to their personal utility maximization, nor can they be expected to do so. From the standpoint of state and society, the egocentric rationality of *homo oeconomicus* must instead be considered irrational and destructive, as the case studies will show. I take the position that top managers are overwhelmed when faced with having to make substantive decisions, because they lack the mindset and experience when it comes to the requirements for rational action. Decision-making situations are complex, and neither legislative nor organizational measures are capable of reducing or controlling this complexity. It must be accepted as a given. What top managers require is a multidimensional set of concepts that provides them with a frame of reference in complex situations going beyond merely their own needs. Their decisions have to benefit not simply their individual professional advancement and monetary gain but also their organizations' longer-term objectives, as well as those of society. To achieve this, top managers should henceforth be obligated to act as critically reflective rational actors[2] and strengthen corporate governance in their companies.

This book consists of four parts. The first part presents 12 case studies from the financial industry, including the former CEOs of Lehman Brothers, Bear Stearns, Anglo Irish Bank, ABN AMRO, Merrill Lynch, UBS, and Royal Bank of Scotland. In each instance, I pose the question as to why the portrayed individuals decided one way and not the other.

In the second part, relying on scientific findings from biology, neurobiology, psychology, and sociology, I investigate the influence that nature and environment have on the specific decisions made by these top managers – in other words, an interdisciplinary analysis. In doing so, I am guided not by a model of naturalistic or deterministic behavior but rather by one that looks at conditioning: Even though top managers are influenced by their individual development, top managers are not per se predetermined. There is room for free will,[3] meaning that there is an opportunity for critically reflective action.[4] In this regard, I also look at the degree to which emotions and feelings influence decisions. I consider these to be essential forces related to individual conditioning rather than elements of rationality, as has been proposed by renowned economists. This is because if feelings were rational, there would have to be reasons behind them, but there aren't any. Feelings are evoked, not reasoned. They do not respond to the better argument but rather are driven by very different forces and thus remain rooted in irrationality. In addition, I address models of psychological behavior in order to better understand the decisions of these top managers. The analysis concludes with a depiction of the interplay between rationality and irrationality in issues pertinent to top managers: egomania, compensation, eroticism, exhaustion, experiences, emotions, empathy, one-dimensionality, successes, agents, and rapture.

In so doing, I pursue the following theories: Top managers become overwhelmed when they are confronted with situations that are new or different, and because of their natural conditioning, they do not recognize these as such. External factors also play an important role, such as social and systemic ones. Rational decision-making still remains possible, even constituting an ideal against which top managers can be measured. However, rationality has to be determined not by criteria specific to the individual but rather by those of critical reflectivity, such as the survival and long-term success of the company and the general public's interest in work, welfare, and environmentally friendly practices. Critical reflective rationality requires a multidimensional set of concepts. Managers are not born with them. Rather, they have to be developed over time, and they need to be taught by university economics departments and business schools. Organizations lay claim to the ideal of critical reflective rationality by creating checks and balances. These act to correct and moderate actions and to systemically promote such values as diversity of opinions and ecological management.

The third part of the book is dedicated to responsibility. Proceeding from the analysis and from the ideal type of top manager, I pose the question of who assumes responsibility and how it can be exercised. The focus is on an interdisciplinary model of behavior and action and on the theory that there is no recipe for swift, successful action in every given situation. Rather, there are several time-tested principles that managers can follow to not inherently be in the wrong – for instance, they can act as a role model, treat others with respect, keep their word, and not demand more than what they themselves can deliver. Moreover, management can be learned. This involves a process whose very roots lie in the family. Schools and youth organizations, and, later, universities and companies, are responsible for developing people into managers and CEOs who rely on a multidimensional set of concepts and make critically reflective, rational decisions. It goes without saying that each individual also has a high degree of self-responsibility, whether for his personal development or for his own actions. These responsibilities are described in detail.

In the concluding fourth part, I take stock of the situation and ask what kind of person is suited to be a top manager, i.e., what is to be expected of the individual, the company, and the environment in order to not only prevail in the complexity of the real economy but to have a positive and sustainable effect.

The book is primarily directed at decision-makers in large organizations, for example, private and semi-governmental undertakings, administrations, and universities, as well as at politicians in the legislative and executive branches, who on behalf of the public create the basic conditions for the (financial) economy and, in general, for civic life. Experienced, powerful CEOs and members of boards of directors and supervisory boards, who will likely understand the analyses presented here, are capable of implementing the solutions proposed. Junior managers, middle-management executives, staff members, particularly in human resources, and consultants are also certain to be interested in them, since these individuals are either seeking similar positions themselves or are acting in a consulting capacity for top managers, thus influencing the business model and corporate governance. And because top managers draw a significant amount of media attention, this book is also addressed to media representatives.

Over the past 30 years, I have continuously held leadership positions. A holistic, differentiated perspective is important to me. This book represents a view from the inside, albeit from one who has not always worked in the financial world. I seek to raise awareness, impart suggestions, and encourage individuals to reflect on their own actions. Moreover, I would also like to generate understanding for the complexities faced by (top) managers.

1 Case studies – How did they decide?

I have prepared 12 individual portraits. Nine of them have to do with top managers of large banks, one with the owner of a sole proprietorship, and two with junior managers. By the latter I mean a team leader or project head with several employees who has a clearly defined sphere of action and is responsible for certain tasks and results. In many cases, this involves a younger executive who has worked in the organization for only a few years. Middle management includes executives who oversee a business branch, a region, or a division or who head up an office or a department. Often, they have already worked for a number of years for the same organization and have at their disposal a large number of employees, as well as two to eight managers who report directly to them. They form the pool from which future top managers are recruited. I consider this category to include members of boards of directors and supervisory boards, CEOs, COOs, CFOs, and division heads, as well as the managers reporting to this level. Accordingly, I place top managers on the normative, strategic, and upper-operational level, where they have the greatest amount of influence with respect to their organization's direction, shape, and achievement of objectives.

The case studies cover important stations in the professional lives of the 12 protagonists. All information was obtained from publicly available sources. Attention is focused on their careers and the decisions they made in the wake of the financial and banking crisis in 2007. At the conclusion of each portrait, I ask why they decided the way they did in a given case. In the main chapter, I analyze various motives and causes that may shed light on their actions.

1.1 John Thain, Merrill Lynch/Bank of America

John Thain (born 1955) attended the Massachusetts Institute of Technology (MIT), where he studied electrical engineering. He obtained an MBA from Harvard University. After completing his studies, Thain took a position with Goldman Sachs in the financial services department before moving on to investment banking. He was eventually promoted in 1994 to CFO. He then left when he failed to be named to lead the firm and moved to the New York Stock Exchange, where he advanced to become CEO. Here he undertook drastic cost-cutting measures, implemented the switch to electronic trading, and took the company public. In 2007 Thain moved to Merrill Lynch where he received a signing bonus of USD 15 million and stock worth USD 68 million.[5]

Known as a cool, calculating problem-solver, Thain implemented rigorous cost-cutting at Merrill Lynch as well, firing hundreds of employees and slashing salaries. At the same time, however, he hired two, high-ranking investment bankers from Goldman Sachs for a combined total of USD 68 million and had his office renovated for USD 1.2 million.[6] As the crisis on the financial markets was becoming evident with the takeover of Bear Stearns by JP Morgan Chase in March 2008, Thain succeeded in divesting the firm's most toxic securities and obtaining urgently needed capital. That fall, following the collapse of Lehman Brothers, he was able to sell Merrill Lynch to Bank of America, securing himself and other top managers bonuses totaling USD 3.4 billion. After Merrill Lynch's stock price plummeted despite the takeover and the public became aware of the costs for the office renovations and the staggering bonuses despite poor business performance, Thain was fired on January 22, 2009.[7]

Why did Thain decide to renovate his office for USD 1.2 million and pay himself and others bonuses worth billions of dollars despite massive losses?

1.2 Richard Fuld, Lehman Brothers

Richard Fuld (born 1946) studied at Boulder University in Colorado and at New York University, where he obtained his MBA. He began his career at Lehman Brothers in 1969 as a commercial paper trader, at a time when messengers carried certificates from office to office. Fuld worked his way up the ladder, from dynamic trader to successful CEO. One might say that his career came to symbolize the investment banker with a disproportionate bonus, since he earned roughly USD 40 million annually between 2000 and 2007. He headed the company for 14 years, from 1994 to 2008, and was considered to be one of the financial world's most competent and experienced CEOs.[8] During his reign, Lehman's profit soared from USD

113 million in 1994 to USD 4.2 billion by the end of 2007. During the same period, the firm's stock price rose twentyfold. Fuld identified himself with his investment bank, calling it his "oxygen."[9]

In the 1980s, a battle unfolded for control of Lehman, which Fuld was able to follow at close range. Two senior partners – Lewis Glucksman, head of trading, and Peter Peterson, head of investment banking – engaged in a fierce clash for sole control of the bank. Glucksman outmaneuvered his opponent and emerged victorious, but this resulted in a broad rift between the traders and the more traditional bankers. The firm became so weakened that it was acquired by American Express in 1984. The loss of independence and income and the harm to the company's image were a heavy blow to the partners, including Fuld. It was at this time that he allegedly said that he would never again tolerate this kind of power struggle at the expense of the company.[10] It would take 10 years for Lehman Brothers to once again become an independent bank, and Fuld was made CEO.

Fuld was an imposing figure. At headquarters, he was known for his steely expression and his blunt, emotionally colorful language, for example, in referring to competitors or a manager's clothing. He was nicknamed the "Gorilla" and was a sought-after speaker and interview subject. On the other hand, he was not known for being a partier or a big networker.

Over the years, there were a number of changes at the top of the company. In 1996 COO Christopher Pettit, a friend and ally of Fuld, was forced out because the two could not agree on reorganizing how the company was to be run. Fuld did not name a new COO for six years. In the interim, Michael F. McKeever, head of investment banking, left the firm following run-ins with Fuld. John Cecil, CFO until 2000, experienced a similar fate and was demoted after falling out with Fuld. Critics of Fuld, like Michael Gelband, known for his brilliant risk analyses, and Madelyn Antoncic, also left the company.

In 2004 Fuld appointed a COO loyal to him, Joseph M. Gregory, who made it his mission to keep all problems at a distance from Fuld. Meetings with Gregory were known for being a kind of "monologue."[11] He could give extensive lectures on how to prepare meeting minutes or about the suit a meeting participant was wearing. He sought to be informed about possible contrary opinions prior to each meeting. The sole business of meetings was to rubber-stamp deals, as participants later recalled. Whereas Gregory valued unity and discipline at headquarters, he also sought to promote internal competition in areas where profits were at stake. He deliberately encouraged rivalries between the New York and London offices. These two divisions fought tooth and nail for better results, higher bonuses, and greater influence with the CEO and COO.

Even after the first signs of the crisis became apparent following the takeover of Bear Stearns by JP Morgan Chase, Fuld believed that Lehman had sufficient equity. When contacts were initiated with General Electric and Berkshire Hathaway, this was apparently more for the purpose of bolstering the market's faith in Lehman than for borrowing money.[12]

On September 15, 2008, 158 years after its founding as a brokerage, Lehman Brothers was forced into bankruptcy. Former U.S. Treasury Secretary Henry M. Paulson, Jr. said he was not prepared to use taxpayer dollars to bail out the firm. However, just six months earlier, the administration had provided USD 29 billion in financing for the purchase of the investment bank Bear Stearns by JP Morgan Chase. Ben S. Bernanke, chairman of the U.S. Federal Reserve, insisted that there was nothing that the administration could do to prevent Lehman's collapse.[13] Fuld had earlier warned that driving his company into bankruptcy could unleash a "financial Armageddon."

In 2006 Fuld was named by the magazine Institutional Investor as the top CEO in the "Brokers & Asset Managers" category, but once the economic crisis broke out, cable broadcaster CNBC placed him at the top of the list of "Worst American CEOs of All Time."[14]

It has been established that Fuld was repeatedly warned by Mike Gelband, head of capital markets at Lehman, that a bubble was threatening to burst.[15] Why did he ignore these warnings and call upon Gelband to be less risk-averse?

1.3 Marcel Ospel, UBS

Marcel Ospel (born 1950) was trained as an investment advisor and eventually obtained a degree in business administration. He began his career in 1977 at the Swiss Bank Corporation. In 1980 he joined the newly formed investment banking department in London, where he became fascinated with the Anglo-American style of investment banking, and moved on to

New York one year later. In 1985 Ospel took a position with Merrill Lynch in Zurich, before returning to the Swiss Bank Corporation in 1987 to run the securities trading department. In 1989 Ospel began working again in investment banking, and in 1990 he took over international operations together with Hans de Gier.

In order to create an investment bank that could challenge the Wall Street titans, Ospel pursued a strategy that focused on acquisitions: Brinson Partners (1994), S.G. Warburg (1995), and Dillon, Read & Co. (1997) were acquired for a total of several billion dollars. This strategy culminated in the merger of Swiss Bank Corporation with Union Bank of Switzerland (UBS) in 1998. As a result, Switzerland's largest bank could now concentrate on the highly profitable segments of investment banking and wealth management. The plan to conquer Wall Street was set to commence. Ospel initially served as CEO of UBS. Following the resignation of Matthias Cabiallavetta in the aftermath of the collapse of the hedge fund LTCM, which cost UBS billions, Ospel was named chairman.[16]

In 2001 John P. Costas was appointed CEO of UBS's investment banking division. Under his leadership, earnings rose year by year. In 2004 his traders contributed 46% to the firm's total profit. One year later, Costas suggested to Peter Wuffli, CEO of UBS, that the firm set up a private hedge fund called Dillon Read Capital Management (DRCM) with Costas at the helm. While it has never been demonstrated whether all directors were completely behind the project,[17] it is clear that Ospel immediately agreed to it. His decision may have been influenced by the fact that Costas was in discussions at the time about taking over as head of Merrill Lynch. Ospel didn't want to lose Costas.

DRCM began operations on July 1, 2005. Costas brought two of his deputies on board, Mike Hutchins and Ken Karl, along with 80 top traders. Whereas most private hedge funds have to raise their own resources, UBS generously funded DRCM to the tune of USD 3.5 billion. Costas, Hutchins, and Karl each earned USD 30-50 million annually. They took a share of profits without having to participate in losses – another factor setting DRCM apart from other private hedge funds.[18] In 2006 DRCM generated net profits of roughly USD 1.2 billion. Its 230 employees received bonuses averaging USD 1 million. These bonuses created strong tension with the investment banking division, whose employees sought to copy DRCM's success.

In February 2007, DRCM traders – among them, John Niblo – identified a shift in trends on the U.S. subprime market. Niblo realized that more and more houses were being offered for sale to fewer and fewer buyers.[19] In March, DRCM began selling off mortgage-backed securities. At the same time, its traders notified their colleagues in the investment banking division, but the latter didn't believe that subprime business was coming to an end. Apparently, the investment banking division's management, under the leadership of Huw Jenkins, a former equities trader, feared that impending write-downs to its portfolios would cost the division its status as No. 3 behind Merrill Lynch and Citigroup, along with their bonuses, and that they would lose the competition with DRCM.

There is no doubt that UBS senior management was notified about the threats emanating from the subprime market. Klaus Wellershof, chief economist at UBS Wealth Management & Business Banking, sounded alarms as early as 2006.[20] Rolf Bögli, COO of U.S. operations, twice flew to Zurich to warn the firm's heads about the risks associated with mortgage business in the U.S., but his warnings went unheeded. Walter Stürzinger, chief risk officer at UBS, ordered an investigation of the DRCM portfolio after learning about the write-downs and the conflict between Costas and Jenkins. But as long as profits were still being made, the UBS board, which was dominated by Ospel, refused to get out of this lucrative business. Euphoria continued to prevail, and in April 2007, the UBS board decided in favor of the investment banking division.

By May, DRCM was out of business, with one half of its employees being integrated into the investment banking division. Costas and his closest associates left UBS with extremely generous, eight-figure severance packages. After generating large profits in 2005 and 2006, DRCM lost roughly USD 150 million in the first months of 2007. The billions in losses that followed were the responsibility of the investment banking division, which continued to do business on the subprime market after DRCM was shut down. In 2007 UBS was forced to announce write-downs totaling CHF 4 billion. Government of Singapore Investment Corporation (GIC) and another investor stepped in to rescue the bank with a capital infusion of CHF 13 billion.[21]

In early 2008, UBS announced a loss of CHF 12.5 billion for the fourth quarter of 2007. Losses from the mortgage crisis in the U.S. now amounted to some USD 21.2 billion. The Swiss Confederation aided the beleaguered bank with another significant capital infusion. In April 2008, Ospel declined to stand for reelection as the bank's chairman.

Why did Ospel create two investment departments in competition with each other, and why did he ignore the warning signs?

1.4 James Cayne, Bear Stearns

James Cayne (born 1934) broke off his university studies one semester before his scheduled graduation and joined the U.S. Army. He began his career in the 1960s selling municipal bonds. At the same time, he was pursuing his hobby of bridge, at which he had achieved an international ranking. In addition to winning a number of tournaments, he represented the U.S. in the 1995 World Bridge Team Championship.

In 1969 he was hired as a stockbroker at Bear Stearns by Alan C. Greenberg, who would later become the firm's CEO. His relationship with Greenberg was always tense. For instance, they clashed in 1975 when, on behalf of a customer, Cayne sought to purchase government bonds that Greenberg felt were too risky. The transaction was nevertheless carried out at the behest of a former superior. It provided to be very lucrative and opened up a new line of business for Bear Stearns. In 1993 Cayne succeeded Greenberg as CEO and in 2001 also became chairman.

Cayne became famous for being a street fighter, i.e., a risk-taking, go-for-broke banker. But he was also known for his jovial relationships with employees and, of course, for his passion for the game of bridge. And under his leadership, Bear Stearns also paid the highest bonuses on Wall Street. His reputation as a lone wolf was cemented in 1998, when Long Term Capital Management (LTCM), a hedge fund set up by John Meriwether and Nobel Prize-winning economists Myron Scholes and Robert C. Merton, collapsed. The Federal Reserve Bank of New York stepped in and put together a bail-out package to prevent a larger disruption to the markets. It called on all large investment banks to contribute heavily to the bail-out fund. Cayne refused to have Bear Stearns participate, stating that it wasn't the job of his firm to make up for the professional incompetence of others.[22]

As CEO, Cayne reportedly focused on keeping an eye on the big picture, as well as on internal politics. In this regard, he manipulated the board. Henry Bienen, president of Northwestern University, once complained to Cayne that board meetings left too little time for debate. In response, he was struck from the slate of board members up for reelection.[23] Cayne kept abreast of matters at informal meals and one-on-one talks in his office, where he questioned employees about the state of their deals. Once he felt he had enough information, he decided on his own about how to proceed. Group treasurer Samuel Molinaro and his deputy Patrick Lewis once presented a risk analysis model for each business unit, which Cayne rejected as too complicated without bothering to consult the board.[24]

Starting in 2006, he became less and less involved in day-to-day business, but behind the scenes, he was still pulling the strings. In the summer of 2007, at Cayne's orders, Bear Stearns invested over USD 1 billion in two embattled hedge funds. Greenberg had previously warned Cayne against doing so, since he considered the investment to be a pointless one that placed the firm at risk. Cayne also ignored Greenberg's warnings about the risks associated with U.S. mortgage business. As the two hedge funds collapsed in the spring of 2008 and with Bear Stearns heading toward bankruptcy, Cayne was playing in a bridge tournament.[25]

Why did Cayne ignore Greenberg's repeated advice to get out of the mortgage business, and why did he reject the proposal to implement more thorough internal risk analysis?

1.5   Sean FitzPatrick, Anglo Irish Bank

Sean FitzPatrick (born 1948) studied business at University College Dublin and in 1974 joined Anglo Irish Bank, which at the time was a staid, conservative financial institution. But when FitzPatrick was elevated to CEO in 1986, he began promoting a strategy of servicing credit customers who had been rejected by other banks. This involved not just private customers but also real estate investors and brokers. While other banks required a waiting period of several days in order to run credit checks and analyze possible risks, Anglo Irish made very swift decisions.

In addition, FitzPatrick particularly valued personal contacts. His employees were instructed to recruit classmates, friends, and former work colleagues for mortgage loans. Customers were even recruited at regattas, rugby matches, and other sporting events. One-on-one talks and quick loan approval appear to have been the main reasons for the rise of both the bank and FitzPatrick himself. In any event, Anglo Irish played a key role in the emergence of the "Celtic Tiger."

FitzPatrick has been described as narcissistic and arrogant. But to others, "Seanie" – as he was affectionately known to Anglo Irish employees – was *the* person in the bank with whom everyone identified. FitzPatrick was highly involved in charity work. He built numerous houses in South African townships, sometimes working personally on site, championed handicapped causes, and organized events for charitable purposes.[26]

Within the bank, he was surrounded by a vetted staff of hard-working, loyal lieutenants. In 2005 he resigned as CEO and became chairman. David Drumm, a FitzPatrick acolyte, succeeded him as CEO. As with his predecessor, Drumm was motivated by making money for Anglo Irish and for himself.

The personal component also finds expression in the fact that loans were repeatedly made to the same Irish real estate investors, the so-called Golden Circle. This circle included such famed multimillionaires as Sean Quinn, Brendan Murtagh, and Barry O'Callaghan.[27] When the real estate bubble burst in 2008, the Golden Circle was faced with billions in losses. Anglo Irish collapsed.

In the course of subsequent investigations, it emerged that between 2000 and 2008, FitzPatrick took out personal loans from Anglo Irish amounting to EUR 90-155 million. The loans were then transferred to an account at another bank shortly before the close of each financial year. Ireland's Financial Regulator deemed these transactions to be unethical, but not illegal. Nevertheless, the revelations in 2008 caused FitzPatrick to resign immediately. In July 2010, he declared personal bankruptcy.

Why did FitzPatrick repeatedly grant loans to the Golden Circle?

1.6 Rijkman Groenink, ABN AMRO

Rijkman Groenink (born 1940) was born into a solid middle-class family. It was at high school that he met his first wife, as well as her father, who was on the board of directors at Philips. Spurred by this path of success, he studied law and then later obtained an MBA from Manchester Business School. In 1974 Groenink joined AMRO Bank, as it was formerly called. He received a series of promotions, ultimately becoming a director in 1988. Having reached the top, he was assigned the task of overseeing the merger between ABN and AMRO. From May 2000 to October 2007, Groenink was CEO of ABN AMRO.

Groenink evidently followed his personal conviction and created a culture at AMRO that put a premium on competition. Within the bank, he was referred to as the "Terminator." A macho culture was said to predominate, which over the years made its mark on the bank's corporate culture, including in interpersonal dealings.[28] For many managers, power struggles and career advancement were the order of the day. As CEO, Groenink was convinced that the board of directors and the supervisory board should focus on strategy and leave day-to-day business to the individual division heads. With the 2001 firing of influential directors like van Tets, de Jong, and van den Brink, all of whom were committed to a more conservative understanding of banking, the bank lost an important counterweight to the Terminator. In particular, van den Brink was committed to the ideal of a universal bank, as opposed to purely an investment bank.

An event that is key to understanding Groenink took place in 1987. A passionate hunter, Groenink suffered a serious accident during a hunting trip. His shotgun discharged while he was putting it away, wounding him in his right arm. After making his way in great pain to a nearby farmhouse, he was transported to a hospital, where he was still able to tell the doctors to avoid amputating his right arm at all costs, the arm that he did everything with. Following a coma, blood poisoning, and further complications, he recovered. While recuperating, he vowed never to complain about the accident to employees.

Groenink supported a takeover of the bank by Barclays, but when the decision was made to accept the offer by a consortium made up of Royal Bank of Scotland (RBS), Santander, and Fortis, he elected to leave ABN AMRO. The takeover resulted in the breaking up of the bank: Investment banking and U.S. operations went to RBS. Santander took the large branch networks in Brazil and Italy. Dutch-Belgian Fortis took over Netherlands operations, including, in particular, retail operations. The splitting up of ABN AMRO was met with great resentment by the public, as well as within the bank itself. Managers of the former ABN felt that Groenink had destroyed their life's work. In all likelihood, Groenink felt the same way himself, since he personally would have preferred to have been paid his severance in Barclays stock rather than in cash, as was mandated by the consortium.[29]

Groenink has held a number of positions in charitable organizations, such as the Amsterdam Society for City Restoration and the Stedelijk Museum in Amsterdam. He also served on the U.N. Advisors Group on Inclusive Financial Sectors and was a member of both the European Financial Services Round Table and the Institut International d'Études Bancaires. He has received numerous awards and recognitions, including Manager of the Year in the Netherlands, 2004 Banker of the Year, and Knight of the Oranje-Nassau Order, which was bestowed by Queen Beatrix.

Why did Groenink decide to move unilaterally into investment banking, which led to the decline and later to the sale of ABN AMRO?

1.7 Jamie Dimon, JP Morgan Chase

Jamie Dimon (born 1956) graduated from Tufts University and worked for a number of years in Boston at a consulting firm called Management Analysis Center, before obtaining his MBA from Harvard Business School. Dimon's grandfather worked as a broker, later opening his own office in New York, which he ran for 19 years together with his son. Dimon often spent his summer months working in the family business.

In 1986 Sandy Weill, the future head of Citigroup, made Dimon his personal assistant at American Express. The 30-year-old Dimon had drawn Weill's attention after Weill had read his master's thesis, which Dimon's mother had given to him. That same year, Weill acquired the small Commercial Credit Group, and Dimon was involved in strategic planning from the very outset. In the following years, Commercial Credit took part in several restructurings, with Dimon overseeing them, and made a number of acquisitions, including the brokerage Smith Barney, where his father had once worked, and Travelers Corporation.

In November 1997, Smith Barney and Solomon Brothers merged, and Dimon became co-CEO of the new company. One year later, Citicorp was taken over by the Travelers Group, which at that time held a substantial market share in the areas of brokerage, investment banking, and insurance. The new company became what is now known as Citigroup. That same year, Dimon had a falling out with his mentor Weill, whom he referred to as a second father. The apparent reason for this was that Dimon had refused to appoint Weill's daughter as chief asset manager for Travelers. After being fired, Dimon took an 18-month break to reorient himself, turning down various offers for top positions, including with Amazon.

In 2000 Dimon was hired as CEO and chairman by the struggling Bank One. To underscore his objective of making the bank a player once again to be reckoned with, he purchased a considerable number of shares with his own money.[30] He set the bank on a strict cost-cutting path and implemented comprehensive risk management, which improved its portfolio. In carrying out these steps, Dimon slashed lending to WorldCom, which spared the bank enormous losses when the Internet bubble burst.

In 2004 Bank One merged with JP Morgan Chase. The two needed each other in order to be able to compete with powerful Citigroup and thus with Dimon's rival Weill. Dimon became CEO of JP Morgan Chase. He strengthened the back office, inter alia, by raising the salaries of risk managers to bring them into line with those in the front office. Then in 2008 JP Morgan Chase took over its competitor Bear Stearns. During the takeover negotiations, Dimon converted his office into a "war room" and together with his top managers went through all of Bear Stearns' books. Only after he was personally convinced that the takeover made sense did he agree to it.[31]

Dimon became known as the "last man standing" and the "king of Wall Street." It has been said of him that he is one of very few bankers who know their business in detail. With more than 250,000 employees in 60 countries, JP Morgan Chase has become the world's largest and most powerful investment bank. In 2011 it posted shareholders' equity of USD 184 billion and profits of USD 19 billion.[32] Dimon has become a vocal advocate in the U.S. for lower regulation of banks, having claimed that there is a "witch hunt on banks."

So it came as a shock in early May 2012 when news broke that a trader named Bruno Iksil, also known as the "London Whale" or "Voldemort," had generated losses of more than USD 3 billion through trading in credit default swaps.[33] Iksil had apparently not been acting on his own, as was the case, for instance, with Jérôme Kerviel or Kweku Adoboli[34] at UBS, but rather under the supervision of his employer. Reports about alleged losses were circulating among hedge funds in London as early as April.[35] Dimon sought to dismiss these reports as a "tempest in a teapot." However, in an interview with the television broadcaster NBC on May 13, he was forced to admit that grave mistakes were made by (risk) management. The following day saw the resignation of Ina Drew, head of the bank's Chief Investment Office and one of the few female top managers on Wall Street. In the days following announcement of the enormous loss, the market value of JP Morgan Chase fell by more than USD 15 billion.[36] The media began to raise doubts about Dimon's status as a superstar.[37]

Why did Dimon's risk management fail in the spring of 2012?

1.8   Fred Goodwin, Royal Bank of Scotland

Fred Goodwin was born in Paisley, Scotland in 1958. Like Sean FitzPatrick, Goodwin came from humble beginnings and was the first member of his family to attend college, eventually studying law at the University of Glasgow. After graduating, Goodwin took a position with the accounting firm Touche Ross, where he acquired the professional title of chartered accountant. While working at Touche Ross, he became a director at Short Brothers, Northern Ireland's largest manufacturing concern. Two years later, he helped liquidate Bank of Credit and Commerce International, which had collapsed in the wake of a financial fraud scandal.

Goodwin started his career as a banker with National Australia Bank, where he had caught the eye of CEO Don Argus while handling work for the bank at Touche Ross. Argus offered him the job of deputy CEO in 1995, and Goodwin accepted the post on the spot. Within one year, he had risen to CEO of UK operations.[38] It was around this time, while he was working at Clydesdale Bank, a subsidiary of National Australia, that Goodwin acquired the nickname "Fred the Shred," for his ruthless cost-cutting and fixation on generating efficiencies.

In 1998 Goodwin moved to Royal Bank of Scotland (RBS) as deputy CEO. Sir George Mathewson, the bank's CEO at the time, had ambitions to make RBS a global player. An important first step on this path came in 2000 with the takeover of National Westminster Bank (NatWest), a bank three times the size of RBS, with Goodwin playing a key role. His ability to impress investors enabled RBS to prevail over the Bank of Scotland in the fierce battle for NatWest. Goodwin was promoted to CEO in 2001 and promptly cut 18,000 jobs at NatWest.

While at RBS, Goodwin came to be called a "corporate Attila," due to his reputation as a fearsome outsider in the City of London – a Scot who did not attend a private school or study at Oxford or Cambridge. Within the bank, he was known for his aggressive management style. Those who did not share his views were scorned. He had a "five-second rule," which dictated that his first instinct was always the right one. Once, as RBS's new global marketing strategy was being presented after months of preparation, Goodwin interrupted the speaker after several seconds and said it would never be implemented as long as he was in charge. That was the end of the discussion. On another occasion, an employee of a cleaning company fell from a ladder while working in Goodman's office and broke a small model airplane. It seems Goodman's closest aides were more concerned about their boss's reaction than about whether the worker had been injured in the fall.[41]

Dedicated to continuing Mathewson's vision, Goodwin embarked on an acquisition spree at RBS, starting with Irish mortgage lender First Active and UK insurers Churchill Insurance and Direct Line. In the U.S., RBS purchased Charter One Financial Inc. at a price of more than USD 10 billion, which many considered to be excessive. Nevertheless, the acquisition made RBS one of the top ten banks in the U.S.

The bank's assets and profits soared during this period of expansion. According to reports, the investment banking business was the primary contributor to profits. Leveraged buyouts were another important source of profits, and RBS financed a great number of them. For instance, in 2008 the bank lent USD 9.3 billion for leveraged buyouts, nearly twice the amount of its nearest rival.

In 2005, following the acquisition of a stake in Bank of China, Goodwin began to receive harsh criticism from RBS shareholders, some of whom accused him of megalomania and demanded that he grow the bank more organically. Goodwin again came in for criticism when it was reported that construction of the bank's new headquarters in Edinburgh had cost nearly USD 500 million. In all, Goodwin engineered 27 acquisitions for RBS over a period of seven years.

In 2007 Goodwin met with Rijkman Groenink, CEO of ABN AMRO, whose bank was coming under pressure from hedge funds. Ironically, one of those hedge funds was headed by former RBS CEO Mathewson, Goodwin's ex-boss. Mathewson pressured Groenink to accept the offer made by a three-bank consortium (RBS, Fortis, Santander) over that of Barclays, which was Groenink's preference.[39] Goodwin's interest lay in the Dutch bank's U.S. operations, particularly LaSalle Bank (Chicago). Groenink attempted to sour the deal by selling LaSalle to Bank of America, but the deal with the consortium ultimately went through after Barclays withdrew its bid. The transaction was finalized in October 2007, just as the global financial crisis was starting to unfold.

However, the takeover of ABN AMRO's U.S. operations proved to be disastrous for RBS. First, the size of the deal overwhelmed RBS, and second, ABN AMRO was heavily involved in the U.S. in subprime lending. The bank was further weakened by its U.S. subsidiary RBS Greenwich Capital, which was highly exposed as a result of its private equity lending and its underwriting of collateralized debt obligations. To gain liquidity, Goodwin attempted to sell several RBS insurance divisions, but the effort failed. He also sought to raise capital through a share issue. Ultimately, in October 2008, the UK government had to step in with a gigantic rescue package, purchasing the majority of RBS shares in order to save the bank. In October 2008, Goodwin stepped down at RBS after a number of lawsuits were brought against him and RBS and as part of the rescue package, the government had demanded his resignation.[40]

In December 2011, the UK Financial Services Authority (FSA) published a report on the failure of RBS that was highly critical of Goodwin's management style.[42] In the report, the FSA noted self-critically that while it had previously identified a risk created by Goodwin's perceived dominance, it had failed to require RBS to commission a so-called Section 166 review, i.e. a review by an independent skilled person into one or more aspects of a firm's business carried out under powers set out in Section 166 of the Financial Services and Markets Act 2000. The FSA's review team felt that commissioning a Section 166 review would have sent a strong message to RBS, including its board.

Earlier in 2011, it became known through parliamentary hearings that Goodwin had been involved in a lengthy extramarital affair with a top manager at RBS. The top manager's identity and precise job is unclear, but she is said to be a married woman with children, circumstances similar to those of Goodwin, who has been married for more than 20 years and has children. The woman purportedly worked in the global investment banking department, where she was in charge of several hundred employees, and also held a strategically important management position. Her salary was reportedly in the high six figures. Goodwin is said to have begun the affair in 2007, shortly before negotiations with ABN AMRO commenced.

In 2004 Goodwin was knighted by Queen Elizabeth for his services to the banking industry. In addition, Goodwin received the following awards: December 2002 – *Forbes* (global edition) "Businessman of the Year"; 2003 to 2006 – *Scotland on Sunday*, Power 100 list (top place all four years); December 2003 – "European Banker of the Year"; July 2008 – honorary fellowship by the London Business School. In early 2012, Goodwin's knighthood was annulled, and Sir Fred is once again known simply as Mr. Fred Goodwin.

Why, in the middle of the financial crisis, did Goodwin decide to pay billions of pounds for the U.S. operations of ABN AMRO after having announced in March 2007 that he was no longer interested in making large acquisitions, since there were no longer any deals that were "desirable, doable, or affordable"?

1.9 Jon Corzine, Goldman Sachs and MF Global

Jon Corzine was born in Illinois in 1947. Growing up on a family farm, Corzine spent his youth playing sports, including as quarterback of the football team and captain of the basketball team. In 1969 he enlisted in the U.S. Marine Corps Reserve, reaching the rank of sergeant before retiring in 1975 without seeing active duty in Vietnam. During this period, he received an MBA from the University of Chicago and then started working for BancOhio National Bank, a regional bank.

In 1975 Corzine was hired by Goldman Sachs, and he moved with his family to New Jersey. By 1980 he had made partner, and in 1994 he was named chairman and CEO. His rise is closely linked with bond trading. At the time, this segment was at the bottom of Goldman's priority list, but Corzine's trading in governmental bonds earned high profits, which caught the firm's attention.

Shortly after becoming CEO, Corzine successfully maneuvered the firm through the Asian financial crisis and the collapse of the hedge fund LTCM. He was also substantially responsible for Goldman's initial public offering, although the battle surrounding it ultimately cost him his job, forcing him to leave the firm after 24 years. His adversary in this power struggle was Henry Paulson, who later served as Treasury Secretary under George W. Bush and was thus one of the key figures in the financial crisis. Nevertheless, Corzine left the firm as a wealthy man: Because of his share-based compensation package, Corzine earned USD 400 million from Goldman's IPO.

After leaving Goldman, Corzine, a Democrat since his time in rural Illinois, promptly turned his attention to politics. In 2000, he successfully ran for a New Jersey seat in the U.S. Senate, spending more than USD 100 million of his own money for the campaign. As senator, he was a decisive legislator and advocated numerous bills that Republicans considered very liberal, such as improved access to health care and education, tighter environmental regulations, infrastructure investments, and enhanced security at chemical plants to guard against terrorist attacks.

In 2003 Corzine divorced his wife Joanne, whom he had known since high school. The two have three children. After separating from his wife in 2002, Corzine began appearing in public with Carla Katz, whom he had been dating for several years. The relationship came under criticism, since Katz was president of the New Jersey chapter of the Communication Workers of America union, which represents a significant number of the state's public employees. The couple broke up in 2004, and even though Katz was not married to Corzine, she received a settlement worth millions, including a condominium, a Volvo sport utility vehicle, and a college trust fund for her children.

In 2005 he announced his candidacy for the governorship of New Jersey. He was elected promising to govern the state with the same integrity and entrepreneurial spirit that he had shown in running Goldman Sachs. However, he was unsuccessful in making a significant reduction in the state's debts. Moreover, he decided against reducing property taxes, despite many of the state's residents being in favor of it.

On April 12, 2007, in the middle of his term, Corzine was involved in a serious car accident, suffering injuries that nearly cost him his life. His SUV, which was being driven by a state trooper, crashed into a guardrail at high speed. Corzine, who was not wearing a seatbelt, suffered a broken leg, 12 broken ribs, and wounds to his face. He was forced to spend a number of weeks in the hospital, where, at his own expense, he had a video conference room set up so that he could continue to carry out his duties.

During Corzine's time as governor, there were renewed contacts between him and Katz, who sought to use their relationship to benefit family members working for the state and for union purposes. More than 120 emails and telephone calls between the two have been documented. Corzine failed to prevent them from being published, despite spending more than USD 100,000 in taxpayer money in the process. Ultimately, Corzine lost his bid for reelection in 2009, despite the support of President Obama.

In March 2010, two months after leaving office, Corzine was appointed CEO of the financial derivatives broker MF Global. The firm has its roots in American agriculture. Many farmers used futures contracts in order to sell their goods via the firm. At MF Global, Corzine attempted to put into place the successful model he had used at Goldman Sachs. Under Corzine, MF Global dramatically increased its holdings of sovereign debt, especially that of Spain, Portugal, Italy, Ireland, and Greece. In all, these bonds amounted to USD 6.3 billion. Corzine was betting that they would rise sharply in value in the event of a consolidation of the European market place. Michael Roseman, the firm's chief risk officer since 2008, sounded a number of alarms about the risks associated with this.[43] Corzine rejected the warnings as implausible, and he fired Roseman in January 2011.

The problems at MF Global started with a report by regulatory authorities that asserted that the large number of bonds owned by MF Global were problematic. Even though the bonds had lost very little in value because they had been purchased at favorable terms, the authorities concluded that they constituted an unjustifiable risk and a grossly negligent decision. MF Global was ordered to increase its net capital at once.

The quarterly numbers were bad, and troubles continued to mount for the firm, which was being called a "dinosaur." Corzine felt compelled to tap new sources of profit with risky, even illegal transactions. First, transactions were to be financed with so-called repurchase agreements, i.e., the bonds being purchased were themselves to serve as collateral for loans. Interest on the loans was lower than the yield generated by the bonds for MF Global. Although this practice was apparently widespread, the regulatory authorities had intended to limit or prohibit it where customer funds were involved. Second, customer funds were lent back to the firm through a series of complex accounting maneuvers – in other words, MF Global used these funds to lend money to itself. Since the regulators had sought to put a stop to this practice, the former politician turned to his network and influenced a majority of the five commissioners, with the result that a prohibition was postponed.

On October 31, 2011, MF Global filed for bankruptcy after Corzine failed to find a buyer for the firm. Some 3,300 employees lost their jobs. According to various sources, Corzine himself lost several hundred million dollars through the collapse. He had been working at MF Global for just 20 months.[44]

As CEO of MF Global, why did Corzine decide in the spring of 2010 to take on substantial risk by buying the sovereign bonds of economically weakened countries?

1.10 Marc Dreier, Dreier LLP

Marc Dreier (born 1950) grew up in an affluent New York family. Dreier was a good student, earning degrees from Yale and Harvard Law School. He worked for 20 years at a number of prominent law firms, first as associate and later as partner, earning an annual salary of USD 400,000.[45]

In 1996 he teamed up with Neil Baritz to form the law firm Dreier & Baritz. Dreier was successful here as well, gaining a reputation as a "shark" for his ruthless style of litigation on behalf of his clients.[46] Dreier & Baritz opened offices in a number of U.S. cities. Then, William Federman, a partner in Oklahoma, sued Dreier for improper accounting of the escrow account for one of his clients, and after the two reached an out-of-court settlement, Baritz left the firm. Dreier went on to form Dreier LLP, starting with 30 lawyers in 2003 and reaching 250 five years later. The firm's main offices were on New York's tony Park Avenue. Dreier's clients included TV star Jay Leno and professional football players.

Dreier's criminal dealings began in 2004. He arranged for fictitious loans from hedge funds and pocketed the loan proceeds. The scheme he created required constant forward momentum, much like Madoff's Ponzi scheme. He turned to ever more brazen methods to fleece his customers. For instance, he would commandeer the conference room in the offices of a wealthy New York client and then invite hedge fund managers to meetings there. Dreier would introduce them to one of his attorneys, who posed as the client's top executive. Together, they persuaded the hedge fund managers to buy promissory notes supposedly issued by the client.

However, these notes were bogus, and Dreier's client knew nothing about them.

With the ill-gotten gains, Dreier proceeded to acquire an USD 18-million yacht, artwork worth USD 40 million, houses in the Hamptons and in the Caribbean, and an apartment in Manhattan. The offices of Dreier LLP were said to be like a museum, with paintings by Picasso and Warhol. Dreier threw parties on board the yacht with its 10-man crew, with guests including sports stars and young women.[47]

In late 2008, his misappropriation of client funds became public. Dreier was arrested and later sentenced to 20 years' imprisonment. Prior to his sentencing, he wrote to the judge, "I don't know what gives some men the strength of character to lead virtuous lives for all of their lives, and what causes others, such as myself, to lose their way."[48]

Why did Dreier decide to enrich himself at the expense of others? How did he "lose his way"?

1.11 Jérôme Kerviel, Société Générale

Jérôme Kerviel (born 1977) grew up in the Brittany region of France. In his youth, he was fascinated with sports (sailing, judo). He went on to study at a second-tier French business school, then joining Société Générale in August 2000. He initially worked in the back office, where he helped to administer the bank's computerized database. In 2002 his co-workers voted Kerviel *Trader le plus sympa,* or "coolest trader." That same year, Kerviel was promoted to the front office, where he worked as an assistant to a number of experienced traders. He was responsible for answering phones and maintaining records, and it was here that he developed an avid interest in the trading of financial products.[49]

Over time, Kerviel became a specialist in derivatives trading. He garnered his first success in 2005 when he bet that the share price of German insurer Allianz would drop, which it did in the aftermath of the terrorist attacks in London in July of that year. Kerviel would have an outstanding year in 2007. He created sham transactions that he was constantly concealing. Kerviel earned EUR 43 million for the bank, which amounted to 59% of all of its income from derivatives trading. His colleagues started calling him a "cash machine" and a "star." Headhunters tried to lure him to rival firms with lucrative offers. He reportedly asked for a bonus of EUR 600,000 but received only half that amount.[50]

On December 31, 2007, Kerviel had made a loss of almost EUR 1.5 billion. In order to conceal these, he created eight fictitious positions, whose size however was flagged by the bank's compliance department. The bank demanded an explanation. Kerviel said the counterparty was Baader Bank, a German brokerage firm that he owed money to. On January 9, 2008, Kerviel cancelled the trades, satisfying the compliance department.

However, Kerviel's problems were now starting to grow. He had bet on an upturn in the markets, taking a number of positions nominally totaling nearly EUR 50 billion. The first five trading days of 2008 in the U.S. proved to be the worst start of a calendar year ever. The more the market dropped, the more Kerviel lost. By mid-January, he was again being questioned by the bank's compliance officials. They once more demanded that he provide information about the eight fictitious, purportedly cancelled trades. Kerviel wrote an email explaining that he had made a mistake: the counterparty wasn't Baader Bank but rather Deutsche Bank. When pressed for proof, Kerviel forwarded two forged emails. To his surprise, the compliance department was satisfied with this.

On the weekend of January 19, Kerviel was planning to celebrate his 31st birthday at a resort in Normandy. Shortly after arriving at the hotel, he received calls from his superiors, who demanded that he return to the bank's headquarters. In the interim, Deutsche Bank had notified the Société Génèrale that it had no record of the trades. Following his return, Kerviel was interrogated for hours.

At the same time, Daniel Bouton, chairman and CEO of Société Génèrale, was busy preparing for an emergency board meeting to deal with a EUR 2 billion loss attributable to the subprime crisis in the U.S. Now, Bouton was informed that a young trader had put the bank in additional distress, with open positions estimated at EUR 50 billion. This put the bank's creditworthiness at risk, which could also trigger a panic on the financial markets. Bouton decided to liquidate all open positions despite falling markets. He said it would be reckless and indefensible to speculate further by holding on and hoping that markets would recover. Several of the bank's top traders were ordered to quickly sell off these positions, and they succeeded in doing so within three days.

Société Générale has stated publicly that the liquidation of Kerviel's positions never exceeded 8% of total trading volume on the European derivatives exchanges.[51] However, the bank has not disclosed how many positions were sold and how many were hedged. On January 23, 2008, the bank issued a press release stating that it had suffered total losses of EUR 7.1 billion and that it would have to seek EUR 5.5 billion in new capital.[52]

On October 5, 2010, Kerviel was sentenced to five years' imprisonment and restitution of EUR 4.9 billion.[53]

Why did Kerviel decide not to declare the profits he made from his risky transactions and instead to continue to conceal his reckless methods?

1.12 Anjool Malde, Deutsche Bank

Anjool Malde (born 1984), the only child of a psychologist and an art teacher of Indian descent, completed his A levels at age 17 as the best in his class. He then went on to attend St. Peters College at the elite University of Oxford, where he joined no fewer than 20 student societies, including positions on the standing committee of the Oxford Union, the world's most prestigious debating society, as PR officer for Oxford Entrepreneurs, and as news editor at *The Oxford Student* newspaper. At the end of his studies, he took part in the renowned competition for UK Graduate of the Year, taking second place.[54]

Malde then took a position with Deutsche Bank in its investment banking department, rising quickly up the ladder. He was fascinated with equities trading, as he later pointed out in an interview: "In a single week, I met with a number of CEOs. For one of them, we placed shares worth one billion pounds." The deal made the front page of the *Financial Times*. He also made a 15-minute promotional film for Deutsche Bank's investment banking department for the purposes of recruiting university graduates. Malde was director, cameraman, and narrator.

In 2006, together with friends, he founded the company Alpha Parties, which organized parties for people of Malde's age and provided tips on getting into London clubs. Malde documented his life on Facebook, where he wrote about his interests: "London, Marbella, Las Vegas, tropical islands, financial markets, restaurants, nightclubs, Jacuzzis and saunas". He loved listening to and making music. A number of his homemade videos are available on YouTube, with his interpretations of such well-known songs as "Hallelujah" by Leonard Cohen. He maintained friendships with other "high potentials" and a number of "Graduates of the Year."

On Friday, July 3, 2009, Malde was told to report to his boss. One of Malde's clients had complained after a post appeared on a financial careers website purporting to be from one of their employees, which read "I'm hot, I'm hot." Deutsche Bank investigators traced the IP address to Malde's computer. The poster had apparently first assumed the client's identity and then made the post. In addition, an email was found that had been sent from Malde's computer using an email account with the pseudonym Raj Rocks. After meeting with three Deutsche Bank officials, Malde was sent home. His access to Bloomberg, the lifeline of every equities trader, was also blocked. While he wasn't fired, an internal investigation was scheduled for the following week.

On Sunday, July 5, Malde left his apartment in London City dressed in a Hugo Boss suit and made his way to the exclusive restaurant Coq d'Argent, where he ordered a glass of champagne and headed over to the roof terrace. From there, he climbed over a glass barrier and jumped to his death. According to the coroner, recordings made by closed-circuit TV cameras showed clearly that it was a suicide.[55]

Why did Malde decide to commit suicide?

Twelve portraits. Twelve individual fates. Twelve different organizations and global financial firms. At first glance, it would seem that a link exists between them in only a few cases. But reading the portraits, it becomes clear that there are many common issues, for instance, the extent to which society, markets, and financial systems influenced each manager and whether any human or systemic factors had an impact on his actions. I will go into these issues in detail in the next chapter.

2   Analysis – why did they decide the way they did?

In analyzing the case studies in the following, I am aware that interpretations can be tricky. Some of the decisions lack any unambiguous roots because they are based on complex patterns of behavior and motivations or on specific socioeconomic circumstances. It would be wrong to use the case studies to come up with categories of good and bad managers. Rather, the issue is to make a differentiated argumentation. An interdisciplinary approach should help to uncover certain indicators for actions, which in turn may be able to offer clues and suggestions for a better understanding of (top) executives.

When it comes to management, I am convinced that it is wrong to point fingers at individuals who, in retrospect, made questionable decisions. Hindsight is always 20/20. And we often make the mistake of believing that it simply had to happen that way. However, history doesn't follow a set path – there are too many factors that have an impact on one another, with chance often playing a role. In other words, this is not intended to be a judgment about our 12 protagonists, particularly not a definitive one, but instead an understanding of motives, of possible causes and conditionings, of accompanying circumstances in society and requirements in organizations. A deeper understanding should promote reflection about one's own actions and attention with respect to systemic developments, as well as answer the question of how we can better assign and exercise responsibility in management.

Ten of the 12 case studies deal with top managers – I am well aware that there are unfortunately only few women in top posts in the financial industry and that all of the managers dealt with are men. The focus is on them. I intend to gain an understanding of them gradually, analyzing their actions from a variety of perspectives and with the aid of various models and intellectual approaches. First, I will shed light on the daily routine of top managers (2.1), what conditions them (2.2), and the psychological illusions to which they may be subject (2.3). Next, I will investigate the potential influences of the banking system (2.4) and society (2.5) on their actions. I will then move on to describe the phenomenon of power (2.6) and the significance of the particular situation and chance (2.7) as other important influential factors. The traps facing top managers (2.8) reflect the various types of interplay at work between rational and irrational action.

2.1 The top manager's daily routine – pushing the envelope, biologically

In my discussions with students, I've noticed that many of their statements are based on a process-oriented view of top managers. The way they see it, there are clearly defined phases – for instance, decision-making, implementation, and review – much like the way one envisions that a fiscal year unfolds: Annual targets are set, followed by implementation, then by evaluation, and, once again, by a renewed round of target-setting. While this view is not necessarily wrong in describing management processes generally, it is of little use in depicting the challenges that top managers face on a daily basis.

Let's imagine a day in the professional life of Georg, top manager at a bank, responsible for a global business unit and more than 2,000 employees. This example is fictional, but it is based on my many years of observations.

It is 7:45 a.m. The British Airways Airbus en route from New York has just pulled up to Terminal 5 at Heathrow. Georg feels relatively refreshed, having been able to catch about four hours of sleep. He's just completed a successful business trip. The negotiations with the SEC went well, as did the conference with Andrew, in charge of U.S. operations, and his closest employees. And just before departing, he and Joe, the general counsel, spoke to his employees. He felt that this went well, too. Now he glances at his watch, hoping to make it to the City of London by 9:00 in spite of the morning rush hour. The weekly teleconference with the eurozone heads is scheduled for 10:00. Before going into that, he'd like to speak with Ralph, his chief operating officer, and his assistant. But maybe he could take care of that while in the taxi.

But first things first: clearing immigration. Georg patiently waits his turn in line. He's carrying only a laptop and a carry-on. With any luck, he'll be in the cab in 10 minutes. His cell phone rings: it's his boss's secretary. He has to put her off –

he isn't allowed to use his phone in this area. Once he's beyond passport control, he calls her back. The boss wants to know the latest about how things stand with Case B, a transaction. Georg isn't up to date on the matter right now and doesn't want to speculate. He promises to deliver an interim report with figures by noon. Now he's in the taxi, where he calls Ralph and asks him to handle the necessary clarifications in Case B. Ralph connects him with Sarah, Georg's assistant. Georg goes through the plans for the day with her. Lunch with the head of the investment department has been cancelled on short notice, since he's been called to an urgent meeting at the bank's headquarters. For a brief moment, Georg is happy that he gained some added time. But Sarah has already filled it: The HR business partner wants to meet with him to go over the results of the staff survey and has scheduled the appointment for noon. "Can you call the head of lending in Hong Kong," asks Sarah, adding, "And don't forget to check in with your wife!" Now Georg is staring at his BlackBerry, going through all of the latest emails, answering only the most important ones, moving others to a file for dealing with later, and then forwarding the rest to Ralph or Sarah. Peter, his deputy, calls. He lets Georg know that he's working on Case B and will have the report edited by 11:30. The cab pulls up to the entrance to Georg's office. It's 9:40 – the trip from Heathrow to the City took over an hour. Waiting outside his office are Sarah and Arjun, who reports directly to Georg. "Sorry, Georg, I just need five minutes. I wanted to give you a quick update about how things stand with Case C." Georg waves him in, listens, and then advises Arjun to bring in a representative from the legal department. Ralph arrives, Arjun gets up to leave. It's almost 10:00. Sarah sets up the teleconference. Ralph goes through the agenda for the meeting. "Ralph, please: only the most important issues – objective of the meeting and possible points of friction." The first participant comes on the line – Pedro in Madrid. The conference lasts 45 minutes. No major problems, everything seems to be running smoothly. But Georg really isn't so sure about that. He plans to make another trip to southern Europe. Some things look different up close. But when…? At least the numbers are in order, he reassures himself. Now his cell phone is ringing – it's Harry, the Group treasurer. Georg gets along with Harry quite well. They've known each other for a long time and often converse in German. "How do you think things are going with Matter X?" – "By the way, what do you know about Case B?" Georg thanks Harry – he knows he can depend on him. He glances at the summary from yesterday, drawn up by his people. Nothing special, at any rate nothing that he didn't already know. Peter and Ralph are outside his office, waving the report on Case B. Sarah brings in a tea, no sugar or milk. "Harry just called. He says we should decide about Case B as follows…" Ralph takes notes, makes changes to a paragraph. "Can I send this out under your name?" he asks his boss. "Of course. I know can depend on you!" Georg shakes hands with Peter and Ralph. "What would I do without the two of you?" – "Sarah, is the PowerPoint presentation ready for my lecture tonight?" "A few slides still need to be added, Georg, but we'll have it finished in an hour."

It is 11:45 a.m. Patricia, the HR business partner, comes in to see Georg. It seems to him that she simply appeared out of nowhere. "Hi, Georg, how are you?" "Fine, thanks. You?" All of a sudden, he starts feeling tired. He would much rather have had Sarah get him some wonton soup from the Chinese place around the corner so that he could eat in his office and … oh, right, call his wife. He wonders how his younger son is doing – does he still have a fever? They sit down in Georg's office. Sarah brings in two sandwiches and two glasses of water. Compared with last year, the results from this year's personnel survey are better. Only two departments showed little improvement, in some areas, even slight deterioration. "How do you explain that, Patricia?" "I'm not sure," she says. "With Lionel, it's pretty much the same every year. The steps that you and the others took on the management level don't seem to have worked very well with him. And with Karen, there were a lot of changes on her management team." – Georg's thoughts start to drift. This was the answer that he'd expected. What he really should do is take some time and pay more attention to these two departments. His cell phone rings again. The display shows that the global head of compliance is calling. "Sorry, Patricia, I have to take this!" – Georg agrees to meet with his colleague in the latter's office at 6:15 p.m. Now he starts hoping that the talks with the British regulators this afternoon won't take too long. This appointment is literally giving him a bellyache. He's sure that his people have done every conceivable thing to make a good impression. The supervisory authorities have gotten much more aggressive. They want to know everything, setting deadlines that are impossible to meet without great effort and expense. "Patricia, thank you very much. I have another appointment scheduled for 1:15."

In retrospect, the afternoon went quite well. The meeting was indeed well planned. There were only a few objections, but these have to be cleared up in a week's time. He had to excuse himself from the meeting three times in order to take urgent calls. First, the boss wanted to discuss Case B with him. Then, the CEO wanted his personal assessment of the state of things in Country E. And finally, he was annoyed by a text message saying that a director whom he prized and had nurtured as an up-and-coming talent had given her notice of termination and was moving to a competitor. Was it just a coincidence that she worked for Lionel? He tried reaching her on her cell phone, but got only her voice mail. He wanted to look into this further. He felt awkward leaving the meeting three times, even though Ralph was handling the agenda and seemed to have everything under control.

The visitors left at 5:30, and Georg asked his people to remain in the conference room. "Thank you everyone for your work. Well done." Then he asked his employees, "So where do we stand now? And what are the action points?" The responses satisfied him.

At 6:15, Georg meets with Martin, the global head of compliance. Just before going into the meeting, he finds a message on his iPhone: "Georg, if possible, please call me back at once about lending conglomerate in D. Regards, Brian." Just before stepping into Martin's office, Georg calls Brian, head of the market risk division. They agree to a brief teleconference that evening at 7:00. The talk with Martin is not particularly pleasant. There are apparently several problems in connection with an important transaction. Martin feels that Georg's people didn't do a good enough job of vetting certain contacts and customer names. Georg can hardly believe what he's hearing, but he stays calm and promises to look into the matter. He doesn't want to ruin things with Martin – he's too important and has always been a reliable partner. Their discussion is briefly interrupted when Martin's assistant puts through an urgent call. Georg uses this opportunity to update Peter and Ralph about the new problem and direct that they start looking into it at once. As Georg returns to his office at 6:50, Sarah is waiting for him with a glass of water, along with the presentation for his lecture before the bank's risk committee. "If there's nothing else pressing, I'm going ashore now and will return on board tomorrow," she says. "Sure, no problem. Have a nice evening," replied Georg, who is already engrossed in the text for his lecture. Ralph steps into the office: "I have an initial lead in the case involving the director who terminated. Do you have a moment?" "I'm afraid not. I've got to see Brian in a minute, then I have to go over to the main building to the committee. Do you think I should call her?" "That would be a good idea." The phone rings – it's Brian. … That sounds better than he'd feared, thinks Georg. … He packs up his things, sticks the presentation under his arm, and says goodbye to Ralph. "Don't forget tomorrow's meeting with the front office. Do you have everything you need?" – "Of course," says Ralph. On the way to the meeting with the risk committee, Georg buys himself a sandwich and a soft drink. The committee members are in a good mood tonight. There aren't any delicate questions – only two assignments, and both aren't due until the end of the month. Which is next week.

At 10:00 p.m., Georg climbs into a taxi. He feels a bit wired, he isn't the least bit sleepy. I hope I can get a good night's sleep this evening, he thinks. Tomorrow, I have to be in the office by 7:00 am. He calls his wife. The family's fine. His youngest seems to be recovering from his cold. She asks him when he'll be flying home this weekend. ... Now it's too late to call the head of lending in Hong Kong or Jill, the director. After reaching his studio apartment, Georg writes a few emails and goes through the work schedule for the next few days, thinking about where to set his priorities. He's troubled by Jill's termination, which makes it difficult for him to fall asleep.

Kevin Kelly, CEO of the executive search firm Heidrick & Struggles, describes a typical day in the life of a CEO as follows:[56]

5:45 a.m.	Get up and go for a run. I think while I run.
7:45 a.m.	Call the Shanghai office to check in, scan through my emails on the train, and then jump into a cab and make calls until I arrive at the office at 8:15, when I have a 15-minute catch-up with my executive assistant.
8:30 a.m.	Speak to our Chief Financial Officer for Asia-Pacific, who is based out of Sydney.
9:00 a.m.	Talk to one of our UK-based consultants about a new project we are working on in the firm.
9:30 a.m.	Meeting with Human Resources about a couple of key new hires in Europe.
10:30 a.m.	Preparation for upcoming board meeting with the director of communications.
11:30 a.m.	Meeting with three of our top billing consultants.
12:15 p.m.	Lunch with a client.
1:30 p.m.	360-degree review with external coach/consultant as part of the work we're doing realigning our leadership team.
2:30 p.m.	Call our office managing partner in Paris.
3:00 p.m.	Squeeze in a meeting with a U.S. consultant on a last-minute trip to the London office.
3:30 p.m.	Meeting to discuss strategic reorganization of our practices in North America.
4:30 p.m.	Meeting with the CEO of an important client.
5:45 p.m.	Call to our CFO.

6:00 p.m.	Call with the external consulting firm who are reviewing our business model.
6:30 p.m.	Call with a partner in São Paolo and then another in Encino.
7:00 p.m.	Call company chairman from a cab on the way to the train station. Then more emails to check while I'm on the train.
8:00 p.m.	Get home and my daughter tells me she needs help with her homework.
9:00 p.m.	Executive committee call.
10:45 p.m.	Head of Asia-Pacific calls asking for a couple of extra minutes – I say can we talk tomorrow morning? He says fine, sure, but still end up chatting.
11:20 p.m.	I hit the pillow until the alarm goes off at 5:45 again.

Brady Dougan, CEO of Credit Suisse, talks about a typical day at work:

I don't have much free time, no matter where I am. Yesterday, for instance, I was in meetings until 10:00 p.m. I got home at 10:45, got on my stationary bike, and worked out with my laptop on the handlebars. That way, I took care of my emails, finishing at about 1:30 a.m. Then I went to bed. I never get up later than 5:30 a.m. I usually get dressed quickly, jump in my car, and drive to the office. At the office, I answer emails and make a few calls. Then I go for a run, usually about eight kilometers along the lake. Afterwards, the meetings start up ....[57]

Top managers lead intense lives. The day of a top manager usually looks as follows:[58]

- The top manager spends most of his time outside of his own office, i.e., he's always on the go, meeting with important colleagues from other divisions or representing his firm in front of clients, partners, and lenders.
- In managing his business unit, he relies on loyal, competent managers. He turns to them when necessary, in some cases directly to individual employees farther down the chain of command, in order to get important information more quickly. Sometimes the top manager also receives emails, usually because he is cc'ed, that are low priority for him and thus annoying.
- His actions are usually determined by others. Key individuals and bodies in the firm request meetings or interrupt him with phone

calls. The top manager has to make himself available to listen to and hand-hold important clients, since they always want to speak with the boss and not be passed on to lower-level managers. The top manager is surrounded by staff who put together weekly and daily schedules and thus determine a part of his schedule as well.

- He is rarely able to work without interruption and is constantly being assigned new duties. His day is a series of phone calls, meetings, formal and informal talks, emails, and text messages. He is continually on the move, talking and writing brief messages.
- Unexpected surprises are the order of the day. He is called upon to render an opinion here, put out a fire there. Everyone wants something from him, always with their own interests in mind. His work day begins not with the first official appointment or upon reaching company offices but rather when he gets out of bed and checks his cell phone and BlackBerry. And the day often doesn't end until he turns off the bedside lamp, leaving his BlackBerry switched on since the general counsel is currently in Asia and had already said he would report in about Case B.
- His attention span is short, especially with regard to internal business: People that want to or have to present something to him or need a decision from him would be well advised to be thoroughly prepared but also to summarize the most important points and make pithy statements. They'll have at most five minutes to describe the issue, formulate the request, and provide reasons for it. The top manager can be expected to interrupt these presentations before they are over and ask precise questions.
- Everything has to be accomplished quickly – both advice and opinion about the project. There's not enough time to reflect about it. Decisions are normally made after brief consideration, i.e., spontaneously and intuitively. Many of these decisions are made in meetings with trusted managers, meaning that they are essentially consensus decisions. Critical questions are rarely asked in these meetings.
- The top manager has emotions and feelings. His brain is constantly at work, shifting between intimate, private thoughts and those dealing with business. Time and again, suppressed or forgotten things pop up that are attached to emotional markers.
- His professional and private lives co-exist, since the work of a top

manager doesn't end at 6:00 p.m. or on Friday evenings. Work continues at dinner with investors, at a business lunch, or during a round of golf, as well as at home on the weekend or at the vacation house in the mountains.

The top manager is constantly on the move for his firm, day in and day out, often on Sundays as well. For this reason, many employees and even his own children think that he is never around. He is in great demand, the focal point for everything: when he asks a question, the answer is supplied to him; when he needs to take a trip, everything is planned down to the last minute; when he has an idea, it is implemented. Everything seems possible. And this is where danger lurks: hubris, aloofness, distancing himself from employees and their daily concerns.[59] A tight schedule, a hectic pace, and the feeling that his life is being determined by others may also lead the top manager to seek diversion in order to get away from the daily grind. The top manager may gather with like-minded gentlemen in elite circles or at after-hours clubs for culinary or erotic indulgences. Or he may turn to drugs, take pills to go to sleep or to wake up, drink alcohol excessively, or use cocaine. This behavior is not only damaging to his health and spirit, but it also leads to his becoming isolated from the rest of the world.[60]

And how do things stand with the basic need for sleep? Frequent travel across multiple time zones, long working hours, and constant challenges are neither good for his health nor a sound basis for giving him at least six hours of sleep a night. As shown by the example of Brady Dougan, his body gets taxed when he has to, or wants to, go extended periods on just four hours' sleep. Physical exercise refreshes mind and body. But too much exercise can put additional strain on the body.

Stress is caused by a mixture of intellectual strain, work load, anxiety, and jet lag. When combined with lack of sleep, not enough fluids, and a fatty, sugar-laden diet, stress poses a threat to the entire organism.

Just one week with only four hours of sleep a night can lead to fatigue and exhaustion. When we don't eat, or don't eat enough, we lose weight and become sick. Lack of sleep is hard to see or feel. The body provides hardly any feedback. But the consequences are nothing short of dramatic: First, with increasing lack of sleep, the body loses glucose, i.e., it metabolizes sugar. This is why, when we're tired, we crave sweets in the form of chocolate bars and other sugary snacks. However, the brain metabolizes twice as much sugar. After seven nights with four hours of sleep, the brain receives 6% less glucose, and the prefrontal cortex and the parietal lobe lose as much as 12-14%. It is those very areas of the brain that we predominantly need in order to think, to distinguish between ideas, to differentiate between morally correct and incorrect behavior, and to control our social behavior. Second, lack of sleep is comparable to having a blood alcohol level of 0.1% in the brain. In many countries, like the U.S. and the UK, the legal limit for driving a car is 0.08%. At 0.1%, the average person is likely to suffer from mood swings and emotional over-reactions, have impaired or tunnel vision, and employ flawed logic.[61]

A 2012 survey of 30 executives in Germany showed that most of them push themselves to the limits of their ability to tolerate physical and emotional stress and that they feel overwhelmed, complaining of the lack of room for reflection and regeneration.[62]

Under circumstances such as these, the top manager may act as if drunk: He is emotionally unstable, has limited perceptions, and interacts only with trusted individuals in his personal circle. In addition, he avoids making decisions that require him to exercise critical reflective rationality.

Did Thain, Fuld, and others make some of their decisions in a state of fatigue or even exhaustion? There are many indications that at least some actions were based on such unhealthy conditions.

2.2 Neurobiological findings – conditioned through experiences and emotions

Decisions are at the core of management. The top manager and his managers make countless decisions every day. And because decisions are prepared and made in our brains, we should first look at the events taking place in this important organ.

The brain
The brain consumes about 20% of the energy that we take in from food and drink. It consists of 50 to 100 billion nerve cells, called neurons, and at least twice as many glial cells, which support, protect, and supply nutrients and oxygen to the neurons. Neurons have special qualities that enable them to process electrical and chemical signals which they receive from

sensory organs and pass them on to muscles, skin, and glands. Neurons are comparable to miniature batteries with miniature electrical circuits. They receive electrical signals, modify them, and send them back out. They also produce and process chemical communication signals. Accordingly, the brain is a system for processing information.[63]

Contact between neurons takes place over synapses. Each neuron is connected to thousands of other neurons by synapses. Synapses transmit a received signal to the next neuron either unchanged or after weakening or strengthening it. Under certain circumstances, changes can occur to the structure of certain networks that connect neurons with one another. These changes in turn cause changes in, e.g., perception, thought, memory formation, feelings, or action or motor control.

Signal transmission is extremely fast, i.e., less than one-thousandth of a second, and it is accomplished through neural transmitters.

At birth, the brain weighs about 300-400 grams, reaching 1.3-1.4 kilograms by adulthood. Brain development from pregnancy to adolescence is exceedingly important. Its anatomical development and the dynamics of its wiring take place in stages. The most important stages are the prenatal development of the brain, the first years of life, and puberty. During these stages, the brain is especially sensitive and receptive to environmental influences of all sorts, both positive and negative.

Personality

According to Gerhard Roth, our personality is determined by four factors:[64]

1. Genetic predisposition. Genetic factors differ from one another in their individual composition and in their details. Therefore, in terms of their genetic makeup, their genome, people are much more different than was earlier thought to be the case. While the genetic makeup remains the same in an individual, each gene must be activated and transcribed by processes within the cell, but outside the genome, before it can have an effect. These activation processes determine the time, place, and duration of the effect of certain genes, and they can be altered by environmental influences.

2. Brain development. This involves how areas of the brain develop that are responsible for the psyche. Abnormal development often affects the cerebral cortex, particularly the frontal lobe, or the strength of neural connections.

According to rough estimates, these two factors – genes and brain development – are responsible for determining approximately 50% of our personality, ranging from 20% to 80%, depending on the feature. In particular, they determine a person's temperament and specific talents, including intelligence level. Most studies of identical twins have shown that they are very similar in terms of intelligence, irrespective of the circumstances in which they were raised. Personality researchers estimate that 20 IQ points depend on environment. This means that an individual of average intelligence and average intellectual support will have an IQ of 90 as an adult. However, optimal support can raise IQ to 110, corresponding roughly to the average first year university student. This in turn means that upbringing and environmental factors are by all means significant, even though intelligence is for the most part innate.

3. Emotional experiences prior to birth and during infancy. Prenatal experiences, both directly and via the mother's body and brain, have an influence on the fetus's limbic system. This particularly applies to experiences that trigger serious stress conditions, including excessive consumption by the mother of alcohol, nicotine, or drugs, severe physical abuse, and significant psychological stress. Also of particular significance are the how well mother and child bond and the first experiences with the immediate social environment, such as with the father, siblings, and grandparents. These formative experiences in the first years of life account for roughly 30% of personality.

4. Socializing events during late childhood and adolescence. In addition to the influence of parents and direct family members, the development of our personality is determined by other relatives, friends, schoolmates, teachers, coaches, and teammates. During this phase, we learn to do those things that are considered correct in our social context and in the society in which we grow up and to refrain from doing those things that are considered incorrect. It is generally assumed that this type of socialization accounts for about 20% of our personality.

Our personality is the result of the interplay of genome, brain development, early bonding experiences, and socialization during childhood and adolescence. The factors pervade one another. Each individual is unique due to these four factors and their interplay.

Intellect and reason – feelings and emotions

Decisions are strongly influenced by feelings and emotions. The following depicts the relationship between intellect and reason, as well as between feelings and emotions.[65]

Intellect means the ability to solve problems using logical thinking. Intellect includes the ability to understand tasks within a certain period of time and to solve them with available knowledge. This ability is more or less identical to intelligence. Reason has to do with the ability to recognize superordinate relationships. An individual uses his or her reason by balancing medium- and long-term consequences, as well the social acceptance of his or her behavior. An intelligent person does not necessarily have to exercise reason. Likewise, a reasoning person need not be a priori especially intelligent in the sense of quick problem analysis.

Intellect, and thus intelligence, is located in the brain's prefrontal cortex. This part of the brain deals with recognition of circumstances relevant to action, with the temporal and spatial structuring of perceptions, with speech, and with the development of objectives. Injuries to this area of the brain typically make a patient *un*intelligent. The prefrontal cortex is also where working memory is located. Everything that occupies us at the moment, that we look at, read, or think about, happens here. Working memory is a network that specializes in the rapid assembly of relevant content, but it represents the bottleneck in problem-solving. Intelligent people are able to overcome this by consciously or subconsciously using mnemonic devices and memory aids.

Reason is located in other areas of the prefrontal cortex. This is where, in interaction with other areas of the brain, the longer-term consequences of our actions are evaluated and steered toward social rules and expectations. Other important functions include the deployment of action-related objectives based on earlier expectations and the control of impulsive, egotistical behavior. Injuries here can lead to the loss of the ability to recognize the socio-communicative context. This area of the brain is therefore considered to be the seat of morality, ethics, and conscience.

Feelings include, on the one hand, physical needs – such as thirst, hunger, weariness, and sex – as well as the urge to be socially accepted. These needs form part of our basic makeup, which we can do little to change. Satisfying them creates short-term pleasure and well-being. On the other hand, feelings also include rage, anger, hate, panic, and aggression. We are moved by them, get carried away by them. They are just as inherent as physical needs and just as hard to control. They, too, are associated with an odd sense of pleasure.

Emotions[66] – which are also termed feelings in the narrower sense – include dread, fear, contempt, disgust, disappointment, and dejection, but also joy, happiness, curiosity, hope, aspiration, and exhilaration. Emotions are so-called basic feelings. They blend with one another to make up our range of feelings. They are inherent and affect all people on earth.

However, feelings and emotions differ from each other fundamentally. Feelings emerge as a result of specific situations: disappointment in love can lead to hate, severe stress to rage and anger, but also to paralysis. By contrast, emotions give order to specific events in us and in our world in a very different way. Food that is prized for its flavor in Europe may disgust people in other cultures. Something that makes one person happy may be disappointing to another.

Emotional conditioning

Everything we do or experience has positive, negative, or neutral consequences for us, and these are registered by our brain and stored in our experiential memory. Experience and emotion remain firmly connected. This process begins prior to birth and continues throughout one's entire life. Individual experiences are stamped with emotional markers so that they can be quickly accessed. If we encounter a situation that the brain classifies as familiar or similar, markers are called up from our virtually inexhaustible supply of stored experiences. These messages from experiential memory emanate unprompted, in fractions of a second, and advise us what we have to do or not do.

Emotional conditioning – the images in our heads[67] – usually is not the result of a single event. Rather such events have to recur in order for them to become firmly rooted in experiential memory. This anchoring or "compartmentalization" in the brain takes place all the more quickly the stronger the emotional surroundings or consequences of the events. The first kiss and currently popular music hits remain embedded in our memories. A dog bite can lead to a life-long fear of dogs, and seeing a person dying after an accident or in war can leave indelible impressions and even cause psychological trauma.

Feelings and emotions arise within the brain. The amygdala and the mesolimbic system are the principal locations of subconscious emotional conditioning. It is subconscious because repeatedly positive or very negative experiences are so tightly bound on the level of the amygdala and the mesolimbic system that it is difficult or even impossible to unbind them at a later point. And since this emotional evaluation occurs constantly, starting in the womb, we acquire an enormous wealth of experience over the course of our lives whose details we are no longer even aware of. In daily life, when we find ourselves in familiar surroundings, we thus act intuitively based on more or less automated decisions.

Effect of stress

In stress situations, we often fall back on established patterns. I see this repeatedly in simulation exercises with students and managers. Under new conditions and in a slightly fatigued state, they can no longer call up what they have learned or knowledge that they have successfully applied in tests. Instead of taking time when confronted with new events or tasks to think, identify problems, and then structure possible options for action, they generally tend to take immediate action, pick up the cell phone, and issue orders, just the way they do at work and when in the comfort zone.

In the summer of 2009, I realized in a very special way how easily our brain reaches for that which is familiar and time-tested when faced with stress:

Vacation in England. Underway in a rental car in the scenic western part of the country, toward Cornwall and Devon. For over 30 years, I have travelled by car throughout Switzerland and continental Europe without serious incident, other than a few parking tickets and speeding violations. But I have always driven on the right. As I drove away from the rental agency and into London traffic, I was surprised how easy everything was. I felt that I had quickly adjusted to driving on the left. I didn't encounter any problems until the third day. It happened late that afternoon. My wife and two daughters were in the back seat, while my son sat next to me operating the GPS with the map on his lap. The radio was playing the latest British hits, the women were involved in an intense discussion, and the men ... had gotten lost looking for the hotel. The GPS was acting up. It kept trying to direct us back to the coast. It was an hour past the time that we'd told our friendly landlady that we'd be arriving. Now we were at an intersection. I thought that we had to turn left, but my son disagreed and studied the map. I glanced at my watch. Music and loud voices from the rear of the car, then a short but unambiguous statement – "Dad's lost" – caused me to begin to lose my temper and raised my stress level. Then came clear instructions from my co-pilot: "I've got it, all set, we have to turn right." – "Are you sure?" – "Completely." I stepped on the gas and drove into the right lane. ... "Dad, stop!" My son's order was as if shot from a pistol, and it came at the right time, since I'd just driven the car into the wrong lane. Instead of first crossing the road, I simply made an immediate right turn, just as I was used to doing after years of driving. Approaching us in that lane at high speed, or so it seemed to us at the time, was a car correctly travelling on the left. Fortunately, the mistake had no repercussions. ...

Irritated by the music, the intense discussion that my ladies were having, and the crazy directions, and also a bit tired from the long drive, my brain was confronted with a situation in which it relied on familiar, time-tested patterns: When making a right turn, check for traffic to the left, then turn crisply into the right lane. That is flat-out wrong when driving in England. As long as I was concentrating and wasn't distracted or confronted by emotions, everything went smoothly. But once I was faced with what on the surface appeared to be a relatively low-level stress situation, I was no longer able to act in a manner appropriate to the situation.

Advantages and disadvantages of intuitive decision-making

We make more than 90% of all decisions intuitively and without further reflection, using our knowledge of the matter and our experience in the area. Every question, every problem, and every report instantly and automatically elicits associations, opinions, and judgments. Images of previous similar instances emerge. Emotions associated with them are awakened. The brain compares and then sends messages. Without being conscious of doing so, we decide at the moment on one of many decisions. Right after solving that problem, at least for the moment, the next decision needs to be made. For this reason, it is not surprising that many managers have the impression that they haven't made any decisions on a given day.[68] In fact, they have made many decisions intuitively, guided by their subconscious.

These decisions are based on the totality of the information registered in our brain that is available to us in this situation and at this time in life.

Decisions are conditioned by everything that has made us who we are: a unique person with many strengths and a few faults.

Genes, childhood, adolescence, family, experiences, emotions, knowledge, abilities, etc. have accumulated in a vast repository of information that is now available to us, much like a reservoir. Over time, this lake gets filled with rainwater, groundwater, snow melt, and the valuable waters of many streams and rivulets. Each day water is added, and each day we withdraw some, in the form of thousands of decisions. The reservoir provides an allegory for the registering of events, which facilitates the making of decisions and the management of our daily lives. An individualized lake that is virtually inexhaustible. A lake that makes daily life possible for us through spontaneous, intuitive decisions. Imagine how difficult it would be if we were unable to draw on experience and knowledge. The burdens would start when getting out of bed, with the question of whether we should brush our teeth. If every decision first had to be subjected to a systematic analysis, we wouldn't get to work until noontime. Fortunately, we are conditioned otherwise, and the great majority of our decisions are based on the above-mentioned wealth of experience.

And that which applies to the management of daily life also applies to decisions by top managers: They primarily decide based on their experiences, i.e., intuitively. Along with their genetic makeup, top managers are what they have experienced, suffered, tolerated, worked on, seen, produced, played, spoken, heard, and read, what has made them happy and what has made them sad, whom they have loved and whom they have hated. They are a product of their predispositions and their past, of the family and society to which they belong, of the organizations for which they have worked in the past and for which they are working today.

This totality of information is available to top managers every day, sometimes newly blended or newly organized. It is a constant process that takes place day and night, from the subconscious into the conscious and vice versa.[69] Sometimes the brain plays tricks on them, misleading them into making statements and taking actions that do not conform to the facts. Sometimes they have difficulty remembering things, or exhibit selective memory. However, the fact of the matter is that it is essentially the sum of experiences – i.e., experiences with emotions or mental images – that enables them to make decisions in their daily jobs without conscious reflection.

Our view of the past is distorted. We look at a historical period, inquire into the reasons for a development, and find these facts in history books or political analyses. In retrospect, everything looks simple: It had to turn out that way. But that is a fallacy. The people who had to make the decisions didn't know what the result would be. Maybe they were completely convinced about a certain solution, or perhaps they dithered, doubted, and wrestled with the decision.[70] That which appears to us to be a natural chain of events was in fact and reality marked by uncertainty about future developments.

Application to the case studies

There are good reasons for assuming that several of our CEOs were dominated by their experiences and that their decisions were based – presumably subconsciously – on their predominantly positive memories.

Fuld appears to have been conditioned by a number of experiences. First, by the products and risk management of investment banking, which he had personally witnessed as a trader in the 1970s and 1980s. Second, by the internal battles from 1983–84, which led to Lehman Brothers losing its independence. Third, by his 14 years as CEO, during which he experienced a number of crises that at least in his view he overcame on his own. These highly personal experiences likely led to his undoubtedly unconscious belief that he could deal with every problem that arose and of not needing anyone to manage them.

Cayne was in the business for 40 years, 15 of them as head of a renowned investment bank. He dealt with all difficulties and crises without outside assistance. The risks he took almost always paid off and made him richer.

FitzPatrick: Lending to the golden circle, a small group of powerful real estate investors, was a key element in the economic boom, known as the awakening of the Celtic Tiger. Many companies and individuals became rich, with Ireland experiencing years of economic growth. The business practices of Anglo Irish Bank and the long-term personal relationships with members of Ireland's economic establishment became imbued in FitzPatrick's memory as a model for success.

As CEO of Royal Bank of Scotland, Goodwin took over a total of 26 companies before biting off more than he could chew with ABN AMRO. His bank was thrown into a dangerous imbalance and could only be rescued with government support. The acquisitions that he had made previously had proved to be lucrative, making RBS one of the ten most important banks in the world. With these kinds of positive experiences, he was incapable of refraining from a further take over.

As partner at Goldman Sachs, Corzine transacted bond business with great success and profit. Evidently marked by these positive experiences, he applied a similar strategy at MF Global many years later.

The only one of our top managers who based decisions on more than experience was Dimon: After the Travelers takeover, he ordered up risk profiles for all areas in which the company was doing business. This was because Travelers had suffered heavy losses as a result of Hurricane Andrew in 1992. Even though JP Morgan Chase bought subprime mortgages, it did so to a far lesser degree than comparable banks, and the purchases were always secured by other resources. Therefore, it is not terribly surprising that Dimon wasn't blinded by the apparently bargain-basement price for Bear Stearns. Prior to agreeing to the deal, which was furthermore foisted upon him by Hank Paulson, former U.S. Treasury Secretary, he first undertook a thorough investigation of Bear Stearns's assets and liabilities. And he didn't simply leave this analysis to his employees but instead was personally involved, making sure to stay informed about the decisive numbers.

2.3 Psychological failures – pressure to conform and errors in reasoning

Is thinking and deciding based on intellect and reason all there is? Is *homo oeconomicus*, the rationally thinking and acting individual, a fiction because people can't know and calculate everything and this would take too much time, apart from the fact that because of its evolution over thousands of years, our brain is not created for this purpose?[71]

To economists, rationality means that action has to be consistent and is the logical consequence of individual needs. And as long as a person's needs and decisions don't harm other people, third parties – e.g., the state – should refrain from intervening.[72]

But it is this very harm that occurred in the course of the financial crisis: Millions of people lost their jobs, confidence in the proper functioning of the financial markets was shaken, and a select few got rich. So as to promote an understanding between economists and psychologists, it might make sense to distinguish between econs and humans. The former can't act any way other than rationally, and the latter can't always do so because of their human nature. In my view, this compromise is unsatisfying and, with respect to the improvements that are needed in the financial industry and in management, not very helpful.

Rationality and decision-making behavior from the perspective of renowned researchers

Herbert Simon believed that the following factors limit rationality:[73]

- Possession: People tend to place a higher value on things they already possess than on things they have yet to achieve.
- Risk: People tend to continue to behave as in the past, even at considerable cost, if alternative action is associated with incalculable risk.
- Directness: People tend to place a higher value on events that will occur in the near future than on ones in the distant future, even where the latter, as a consequence of abstract rationality, promise a higher return.
- Contentment: People tend to look at only a few variants, often only two, and stop weighing the respective merits when they hit upon a reasonably satisfactory solution.

Bruno Frey claims that individuals have only limited rationality because they are incapable of stringently adhering to optimal plans. People are often tempted by the moment. In order to combat counter-productive factors like jealousy and resentment, which are incompatible with the model of *homo oeconomicus*, Frey says we need control and limitation.[74]

Reinhard Selten points to the important role of emotions in decision-making behavior. Emotions might, for instance, limit or modify the amount of attention paid to risks. They might also guide the search for socially acceptable solutions or for cooperation.[75]

Gerd Gigerenzer has shown that in many cases, people rely on a heuristic decision-making process, which is based on a narrow basis of information and the application of very simple rules. The most important rule is: "Limit yourself to just a few conspicuous features on which to make your decision."[76] Some of these prominent features include:

- Familiarity: When people decide, for example, to buy a car whose brand they are familiar with, they take very little risk. But if they buy a car of a completely new, still unfamiliar Indian brand, they have to accept some risk, particularly in terms of service and repair.

- Experience: People make decisions based on what provided a satisfactory result last time in a similar situation.
- Elimination: Using a list of potential distinguishing features, people start at the top and then either stop when they are in a position to decide or they strike those variants off the list that are the least suitable until only one remains.
- Contentment: People keep looking until a satisfactory solution is found.

Michael S. Gazzaniga[77] refers to people's moral compass. A stimulus induces an emotion that gives rise to a process of approval or disapproval with respect to a certain decision. Along with other researchers, Gazzaniga believes that we are born with some abstract moral rules and a preparedness to acquire others from our environment. The universal rules that we are born with hold that it is wrong to kill, steal, or cheat and that it is good to help, be fair, and keep promises. On the other hand, moral virtues are not universal but are rather what a specific society values as good behavior.

Gazzaniga distinguishes between five moral modules that influence emotions and thus our decision-making behavior:

- Reciprocity: This can also be termed the "do ut des" formula, "what goes around, comes around." We give something to someone whom we trust or who gave something to us, irrespective of whether this person is related to us. The emotions associated with reciprocity are sympathy, gratefulness, contempt, guilt, shame, and resentment. People automatically reason as follows: "trustworthy" – I'll repay it in kind or I'll take part; "he cheated" – let's punish the cheater; "bad deed" – I'm angry, despise him. – Do you know the ultimatum game? You give player A $10 bill and tell him to split the amount with player B. A must indicate the amount he is willing to give but may not discuss it with B. A and B receive money only if B accepts the proposal. Let's assume A is willing to part with $2. Will B accept? … More than two thirds of all people will reject it, since they feel that the offer is unfair. However, if they were acting as *homo oeconomicus* according to purely rational aspects, they should agree, since having $2 is better than having nothing. Many people in the role of player A offer $4 or even a 50-50 split. Thus, they act reciprocally from the very outset.

- Hierarchy: This module is closely associated with our past in social groups in which dominance and status, from both a social and sexual standpoint, played an important role in survival. Although our modern society claims to be egalitarian, there are always people who are physically or intellectually more attractive than others and are therefore preferred by the opposite sex. Hierarchies exist in all modern organizations. Emotions associated with hierarchy are guilt, because the boss wasn't satisfied; shame, because the boss criticized me in front of others; and anger, because as a result of my mistake, we just missed the quarterly target. Associated values are respect, loyalty, and obedience.
- Boundaries between in-groups and out-groups (coalitions): This has to do with who one belongs to: to country A, to sports team Y, to the white race, to the team with the yellow t-shirts, to the "axis of evil" … People may quickly find themselves in a certain group, but the important thing is that they belong to one at all. Emotions that may be associated with this are: joy (of belonging to a group), contempt (for other groups), rage (at dissenters), guilt (because one doesn't belong to the group or when one harms one's own group).
- Purity: The origin lies in our survival strategy, which aims at avoiding everything that is impure: spoiled meat, unclean water, foul-smelling food, lepers (which is why in the Middle Ages, hospitals were built outside city walls, with lepers being kept separate from healthy people). Disgust is the emotion that prevents us from getting infected. Disgust has a cultural component: children are taught what it means in a particular society and how they are expected to act.
- Suffering: People empathize with others who are suffering. We care for our children, who from birth are dependent on our nurturing for many years. Emotions closely associated with the module are joy when we succeed in helping individuals in need and anger at people who cause suffering.

Stuart Sutherland studied irrational behavior in everyday life, in organizations, and in politics. He described how, for example, the first impression, obedience, conformity, emotions, hubris, intuition, and denial of facts can lead to irrational behavior.[78]

George A. Akerlof and Robert J. Shiller introduced the term "animal spirit" – first mentioned by John Maynard Keynes – into the discussion about rationality.[79] That is how they paraphrase an element of perplexity and inconsistency in the economy. They claim that the financial crisis was triggered by intangible changes in people's heads, by the fleetingness of confidence, by desires, feelings of jealousy, resentment, and illusions:

- Confidence: The cornerstone of their theory is confidence and the interplay between confidence and economic activity.
- Fairness influences wages and prices to a high degree.
- People are subject to the temptation to behave in a corrupt, unsocial manner, which has an effect on how business is done.
- Money illusion: People can be fooled by changes in price levels.
- Stories: Human perspectives are tightly interwoven with our own life story and those of others.

In his study "Freefall,"[80] Joseph E. Stiglitz goes one step further, calling it a fact that people systematically act irrationally and that systemic irrationalities give rise to macroeconomic fluctuations. Irrational pessimism leads to economic downturns, whereas irrational exuberance leads to bubbles and booms, where individuals underestimate risks. He says that they have done so in the past, and when memories of the current financial crisis fade, they will do so again.

Daniel Kahnemann summarizes his life-long research as follows:[81] People have two systems in the mind. System 1 is intuition. It operates automatically and quickly, with no control over itself. System 2 is reason. It requires concentration and work, operates deliberately, and controls System 1. With System 2, our conscious self, we decide what to do. We believe that System 2 dominates all of our actions. But that is an illusion. System 1 steps in everywhere and at all times, taking the lead. This is because using System 2 requires attention and effort and because we can only do those things simultaneously that are simple and don't require special abilities. In addition, the control function of System 2 is slow and needs time for reflection, calculation, or analysis of interrelationships.

Kahnemann reports many cases in which – through the rapid System 1 – we are misled into making wrong or at least questionable decisions. System 1 is an associative machine that makes our actions easier: the first idea, the impression of a likeable person, a familiar reference point, immediately available data, well-known patterns, etc. These are all reasons for rash associations and judgments, which lead to mistakes and biases. System 1 made them available to us. System 2 takes over the misdiagnosis without further reflection and is fooled by its plausibility. If we fail to take time for critical assessment or listen to advice from others, we make wrong decisions.

The consequences of mistakes and biases

In the following, I will go into detail about the most dangerous mistakes, biases, and illusions that we and top managers can fall victim to. In so doing, I break them down into two categories: pressure to conform and errors in reasoning.

a)   Pressure to conform:
- We tend toward obedience and conformity.
- We tend to interpret new information in a way that matches our (value) perceptions.
- Teams, groups, and bodies tend toward groupthink and systems toward herd mentality.

We are accustomed to belonging to a group and to accepting authority, since both are to our (survival) advantage. Conformity is easy for us and gives us a positive feeling: In the bosom of the group, we feel secure and accepted. The top of the hierarchy makes decisions and releases us from the responsibility to do so. Top managers benefit from the respect and loyalty that is shown to them. In this way, they feel strengthened in terms of their status and their decision-making behavior.

The danger of conformity consists of remaining silent when criticism is called for. Facts are overlooked or negated, contradictions are smoothed over, risks are downplayed. The first best solution proposed by the boss is deemed satisfactory, and the only data and facts sought out are those that support your or the boss's plans. No effort is made to think in context, to look into potential conflicts, or to find alternative solutions.

It appears that Fuld and Goodwin employed an aggressive leadership style to vilify dissenters and declare them incompetent, thus increasing the pressure on their employees to conform.

Fuld, Ospel, Cayne, and Corzine ignored information, purportedly repeatedly, that did not match up with their objectives and convictions. They wanted positive thinking, i.e., approval for their projects.[82]

By systematically selecting like-minded individuals for the supervisory bodies of their companies, Fuld, Ospel, Cayne, and Groenink may have institutionalized conformity of thinking and groupthink.

Most of the top managers dedicated their interests and efforts to the financial markets and their competitors, as well as to quarterly results and profits, and in so doing they ignored the long-term survival and well-being of their banks and the interests of state and society. In many cases, this led to pushing forward with investment banking at all cost, to grandiose mergers, to short-term investment and risk-taking, and to spiraling salaries and bonuses. They sought to outbid one another, to outdo everyone else, and to show better numbers and values than the competition. Ospel wasn't the only one who wanted to make his company the No. 1 investment bank. The battle surrounding the takeover of ABN AMRO was waged by the alpha males Goodwin and Diamond from Barclays. This race to the top and for higher profits reinforced the pressure to conform within the respective companies and in the system of the financial industry.

b) Errors in reasoning:

- We tend to overestimate our abilities. Are you an above-average driver? – 90% of individuals surveyed answered yes to this question.
- We tend to view the first idea that emanates from our wealth of experience to be the best option and to defend it in the face of opposition, even against our better judgment or when presented with clear facts.
- We fall victim to the halo effect,[83] for instance, when we encounter a good-looking, charming person and readily also attribute intelligence, empathy, and leadership skills to him or her, or when we believe that a person who is successful in a certain area must also be a top performer in other areas as well.
- Achieved successes delude people into overblown optimism. We don't give enough credence to the fact that success is likely attributable to particularly favorable circumstances or pure luck. In so doing, we overlook emerging risks and don't bother to undertake a thorough analysis of the current situation.
- After a string of positive experiences, we believe we've found a model for success that can be applied over and over to every opportunity that presents itself. In this way, we fall victim to the illusion of the

model, deny the facts on hand, and wave off counter-arguments.

- We focus unilaterally on the end result and pay too little attention to how it came about. Is this representative of the majority of the cases under study? What were the circumstances? Was it chance?

- We unilaterally rely on experts and computers and overlook that experts can make mistakes and computer computations can be based on incorrect assumptions. In so doing, we don't think ourselves and fail to review the data.

- We love plausible stories and let ourselves be misled into not questioning them, nor obtaining background information, such as numbers.

- We reason with what our brain quickly provides us – Kahnemann would refer to System 1, which tries to overload us. However, the obvious answer is not always the right one. We have to bring ourselves to rethink immediately available information and look for other solutions.

- We are averse to loss, which means that we're prepared to accept increased risk when threatened with a loss. Just like a gambler at the casino who has already lost a lot of money, we raise the stakes and risk more instead of quitting and keeping the loss in check.[84]

I haven't listed all possible errors in reasoning,[85] just those that play a role in our context. The examples show that we are constantly exposed to the risk of following dubious impressions and making rash decisions. If we don't pay attention and are insufficiently aware of the mistakes, biases, and illusions that we can be taken in by, we act unreasonably.

In several of our cases, there was either a lack of a systematic, reflectively rational decision-making process or one or more errors in reasoning were made.

Our CEOs may have overestimated themselves and their abilities. People who feel powerful and earn a lot of money are more strongly exposed to hubris than an average citizen is in the estimation of their driving abilities.

Fuld, Thain, FitzPatrick, and the others were undoubtedly shaped over many years by the positive experiences at the top of their banks. Their optimism probably misled them into following the first thing that occurred to them or abandoning themselves to the illusion of a model of their success. They fell victim to their own halo effect and their own evaluation of plausibilities.

With Ospel and Corzine, loss aversion may have played a role: Instead of acting more cautiously or putting an end to risky activities, they took even greater risks. Ospel's actions following losses in connection with U.S. mortgage business, and Corzine's transactions to procure capital for MF Global, serve to support this hypothesis.

Our top managers were apparently unaware of any of the possible errors in reasoning applicable to them that could have interfered with their decisions. And because institutional control mechanisms and an organizational culture of transparency and openness were undoubtedly lacking, there was no opportunity to make corrections.

Natural errors in reasoning reveal a paradox: On the one hand, top managers are exposed to them and "suffer" from them in the form of the mistaken actions that they cause. On the other, errors in reasoning reinforce patterns of behavior that are typically expected of top company executives. Top managers – good looking, exuding confidence, looking to the future optimistically, convinced of their own abilities and the power to bring their own plans to fruition – all too easily buy into their own self-assurance and persuasiveness. At the same time, they dupe their surroundings. At first glance, it indeed seems a paradox, but upon closer study it is obvious. Predispositions developed over the course of evolution that are dormant in us have the latent ability to mislead us into making mistaken, erroneous decisions. But this very tendency toward self-endangerment amplifies the power of top managers to mislead, in that they strengthen their own self-confidence and raise their credibility in the eyes of others. Top managers benefit from the errors in reasoning that take place in their companies:

- Executives and employees fall victim to the halo effect.
- Staff members allow themselves to be misled by the strategy of the top manager, which is associated with earlier successes, positive end results, and plausible stories.
- Experts have reviewed the strategy of the top manager and declared it to be the right one.
- Using mathematical calculations and computer simulations, optimistic prognoses are created to implement the strategy.
- Management, the board of directors, and the supervisory board are presented with myriad figures and reports that back up their strategy.

The lone negative opinion of an analyst is so far-fetched that the listener can only laugh.

- Their optimism motivates employees to support them with all of their efforts in implementing their strategy.

If we consider that "every person of every rank is always willing to believe in that which is to their advantage" (Stefan Zweig), [86] and also take into account the pressure to conform, it becomes clear that the door is wide open to mistaken, biased, or illusionary decisions. The drive to conform and potential errors in reasoning cannot explain all of the decisions of our top managers. But they probably facilitated, supported, and even fatally sanctioned their actions.

2.4 Systemic influences – culture of meritocracy, cohesion, willingness to take risks, and isolation

Top managers are part of an organization. They both leave their mark on it and are influenced by it. Certain organizations are characterized by, among other things, dress and language. In the banking sector, one is expected to come to work in a suit. The last day of the workweek is considered "casual Friday," the only day on which managers come to the office without wearing a tie. Designations and abbreviations that are completely normal and familiar to long-time employees sound like a foreign language to customers. For example, hidden behind a name like CDO is the sophisticated bundling of banking transactions, whose effects for normal customers are very difficult to understand.

The organization, which also includes a bank, is an autopoietic system, since it is self-created, operates independently, and serves as a means for carrying out a variety of often competing purposes: For employees, it is a means of earning a living and perhaps also obtaining professional satisfaction. For owners, it is a means of achieving a return, but it can also contribute to the formation of a personal identity. For consumers, it is a means of satisfying their needs, for example. For the state, it is a means of generating tax revenues. In other words, an organization serves a variety of purposes and a variety of motivations for individual action.[87]

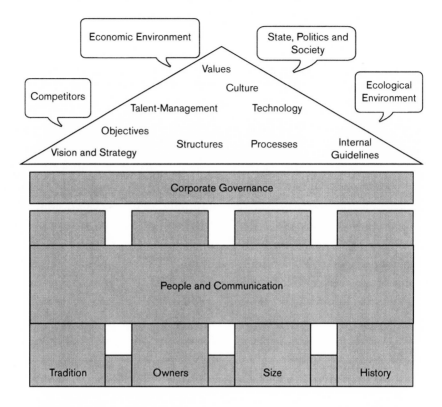

Figure 1: The Organization

No organization is autarkic. Every organization is subject to external influences that prompt it to act. At the same time, it has an influence on the world around it, particularly its market and its competition. By virtue of its very existence, it is paid heed to, and other organizations and their representatives come into contact with it in a variety of ways.

Every organization is based on a specific history, which belongs to the shared "genotype." When decisions are being reached, reference is made to this history, such as in sentences like "That was never common practice with us" or "That has always been one of our company's values." The organization's history is ever-present and tangible on a daily basis.

Organizational culture

In addition to diverse factors like history and tradition, communication between individuals has an important influence on organizational culture. Communication is the key to understanding an organization's culture. It takes place everywhere and at all times and generates effects: Top management communicates visions, strategies, missions, and values. Whether these are accepted, cherished, or criticized depends on the manner of communication, as well as on the organization's inner workings. These inner workings are shaped by middle and lower management and their teams. That is where the most interesting stories are told. Only roughly one third of them relate to concerns that top management considers to be a priority. Two thirds of the time, discussions have to do with other individuals, such as "Did you hear that A stopped in to see B," "C told me that D was transferred," "X gave Z a warning," etc. One can dismiss this as gossip, but it does take place, and it reveals the issues that employees are particularly concerned about.

Middle and lower management and their employees are the bearing elements in a firm: They produce, sell, meet customers, and generate profits. But they are also like molasses, since they access and implement in their daily work only that information that is useful to them and that they like. They are often resistant to change, and it is not always easy to please them. In view of neuroscientific findings, this attitude toward change management is not surprising. As is well known, we tend to prefer the tried and trusted over new ways of doing things. We don't like to break our routines and venture into uncharted waters. Despite internal expressions of dissatisfaction and resistance, top management is only rarely criticized or opposed openly. Obedience and conformity are more common than challenges to a recognized, likely successful authority. In other words, as long there are no dramatic changes, like widespread firings or the closing of branches, the reaction tends to remain hidden. Disapproval usually reveals itself in smaller irregularities, such as missed appointments, incomplete reports, or work-to-rule. Moreover, the organization's inner workings play out in the area of departments and teams, which generally remain out of the sight of top management in larger organizations, unless their representatives seek out direct contact with the so-called base.

Social media, like Facebook, Twitter, and other IT platforms, have accelerated communication. As a result, information reaches a large circle of recipients more quickly than was the case just several years ago. For example, the extent of the Arab Spring in 2011 would have been inconceivable without social media, and one year later, the filling of the top positions at Deutsche Bank would not have become known to all employees world-wide within just a few hours – this was not top management's intention. In particular, junior managers of Generation Y are nearly constantly online with friends and work colleagues. All kinds of news, especially hot stories, spread rapidly and unchecked. Top managers – and the communications professionals in their firms – would be well advised to include this unstoppable trend in their strategies.

Special banking culture

How do matters stand with the special organizational culture that has characterized investment banks in recent years? I have identified the following elements of this banking culture:

- Meritocracy: Individuals are judged by their performance, which is measured – especially in the front office – by the amount of profit generated. This is associated with the willingness to accept long working hours and to go the extra mile for the firm. Among other things, this leads to a culture of performance and competition among individuals. The objective is to prove to oneself and to others what one is capable of. Higher bonuses and promotions make it possible to show what one has accomplished. Personal recognition and attention are the result of all of these efforts. Deutsche Bank's motto, "A passion to perform,"[88] is closely associated with meritocracy. Performance is indispensable: Without performance, there are no results and no profits. On the other hand, there is a risk that we are talking only about the goal. However, performance is not merely the end result attributable to the efforts on a given individual. Performance is also based on the interplay between many employees and on favorable conditions on the market, such as with regard to customers or competitors, as well as on the judgment of how it was achieved.[89]
- Cohesion: This means a certain group's sense of togetherness and solidarity, for example, that of a team of traders. Because of long working days, risky transactions, and reciprocal relationships, a role and relationship system comes into being, which can lead to internal tensions but also, toward outsiders, to a strong feeling of identification. Each person is in direct competition with all of his or her colleagues but at the same time a member of an informal affiliation of like-minded individuals. Cohesion is recognizable through a special language with abbreviations, similar patterns of behavior, codes for

individual products, and nicknames for their role models, usually top managers. It feels good to belong to these street fighters (women are rarely to be found in this environment) and to be recognized by them. By contrast, diminished work efforts, lower profits, or displeasing comments may lead to exclusion from the group and thus to demotivation and to loss of recognition.

- Willingness to take risks: This involves aggressively exploiting opportunities in areas that promise quick profits. It is not that risks are simply ignored. Rather, the prospect that a stock price will rise sharply or that a deal can be concluded at once is considered an opportunity to be seized due to the expected quick profit. A fundamentally optimistic attitude and positive thinking promote the willingness to take risks, as does similar behavior by colleagues that one feels allied with. Statements by top managers, who prize risk-taking as a virtue and see it as guaranteeing the bank's success, reinforce this behavior. Willingness to take risks leads to uncooperative behavior, as was shown by a study at the University of St. Gallen that looked at the behavior of 27 professional traders working at Swiss banks and at hedge funds. In the computer simulation, the bankers' behavior was less cooperative than that of psychopaths[90] or the control group. Of the 40 moves by the traders, on average more than 12 were uncooperative. Psychopaths, who lack empathy, opted for only 4.4 uncooperative moves. The figure for the control group was 0.2.[91]

- Isolation: Meritocracy and the willingness to take risks are aimed at short-term profits. Individual traders are eager to keep important information to themselves in order to make the sought-after profit all by themselves. Interventions by the back office, particularly by a risk manager or a control department, are viewed as meddling and counterproductive. This leads to the silo effect: Entire departments isolate themselves from one another and show themselves to be uncooperative.[92]

This particular culture, which is unique to investment banking, first of all promotes conformity: The individual has the urge to belong to a certain elite, to think less critically, to seal him- or herself off, and to act solely in the pursuit of profits. Second, it exposes a lack of cooperation, which leads internally to silo behavior and to disengagement from the outside world.

Third, it appears to attract a special type of person, one who allows him- or herself to be socialized and instrumentalized in this overheated context.

Application to the case studies

Our case studies document the significance of this special organizational culture in investment banking.

Anjool Malde, Jérôme Kerviel: Although the cases are different in many ways, they are very similar in terms of the motives of the two junior managers. They seem to have been marked, as was the case to an even greater degree with Marc Dreier, by the drive for prestige and status. That may have been the incentive for joining an investment bank. However, they were not motivated by money alone, which confers status, but rather primarily by obtaining recognition from established traders and colleagues. Thus, they evidently sought respect through their performance and wanted to work alongside the Big Boys. Even though ultimately they are responsible for the actions, they were nevertheless shaped by this special organizational culture and can be seen, at least partly, as victims of that culture.

Fuld, Cayne, Groenink, and Goodwin appear to have created a street fighter culture in which, on the one hand, under the motto of positive thinking, the objective was aggressive expansion and profits but, on the other, dissent was nipped in the bud.[93] This could have led to a loss of reality and to an out-of-touch management style disconnected from the suggestions and criticism of the base. The nicknames given to them speak for themselves: Gorilla, Terminator, Attila. This evidently was in celebration of a macho culture and a cock-of-the-walk mentality, which was suited to demanding that underlings work long hours, engage in aggressive competition, and take risks, as well as to promoting isolation and lack of cooperation.

Fuld, Ospel, Cayne, Groening, and Corzine seemed to have sought a harmonious organizational culture. However, they successively eliminated critics and placed like-minded people in top management. Diversity of opinion and discussions in management committees and on management and supervisory boards were clearly not desired, since these could trigger internal trench warfare and interfere with the speed of expansive strategies and profit maximization. By promoting trusted minions, they at the same time purchased their loyalty. They were able to lead and control their banks at their discretion by means of rubber-stamp management boards and supervisory boards, as well positive-thinking management committee members.[94]

When Fuld promoted aggressive competition between his investment departments in New York and London, and when Ospel created two investment institutions operating independently of each other, they presumably reinforced both the willingness of these areas to take risks and their isolation from risk management and from internal firm controls.

2.5 Sociological aspects – associative mainstream, dissociative inequality

The decisions made in the 12 case studies all took effect during the last five years. For this reason, it makes sense to take a look at political and social trends over the past 10-15 years in order to shed light on the influence they had on our case studies. I am aware that it would be impossible for me at this point to depict in just a few sentences the complex reality in Western society. Instead, it should be possible to point out trends that aid in a better understanding of the decisions made in the financial world.

Politics, economy, and media

Politicians in most parts of the Western world aim to offer the economy a stable foundation and to work toward or expand a just social partnership. Interference in the so-called free market economy and controls put in place by the legislature in individual industries are viewed as unwelcome, since they may threaten the free flow of capital, profit maximization, and corporate liberty.

In wide sections of the economy, particularly in the financial world, thinking focuses on short-term shareholder value. The publication of quarterly results, ratings, analyst reports, stock exchange barometers, etc. are an expression of the effort to improve profits, which, as many are convinced, benefits not just shareholders but ultimately also the entire economy, the state through higher tax revenues, and the individual. Banks pay high salaries – or top managers, even 100 times that of a simple employee – but in return demand very long working hours and the willingness to work globally. Economics and management science have supported these trends by clinging to the model of *homo oeconomicus* and by mathematizing the academic training of financial experts and managers, while at the same time ignoring *homo sapiens* in all of its diversity.[95]

Many people in the West – but by no means all! – live in relative comfort compared with earlier decades, let alone centuries. For many, the focus is on the pursuit of personal happiness. The enormous variety of leisure activities and the virtually unlimited ways to receive information or exchange it with other people around the globe are both a blessing and a curse. On the one hand, they offer individual freedoms that were formerly inconceivable. On the other, they add another level of complexity, which can unsettle or destabilize individuals.

The media operate under increasing cost pressure. The influence of the Internet continues to grow, and it is pushing aside print and TV media. Key words like "sex sells" and "infotainment" illustrate the trend toward focusing on individuals, entertainment, and short-lived current events. Media garner attention and improved circulation or viewer ratings primarily through events that the populace finds compelling at any given time. In the process, the focus may be on an individual, a bank's quarterly results, or a stock's crash. There remains little room for background information or commentary to explain the development of an organization over a number of years. Also, this doesn't meet with wide interest, which boosts sales. In this sense, the only thing that matters today (and that will be forgotten by tomorrow) are headlines like "Manager of the Year," "No. 1 Banking CEO," "Top Annual Result." The same is true for a disloyal top athlete or the "precipitous fall of top manager X."

Interaction between mainstream and management

There is an interrelation between top managers and sociological trends: They are designated by the media as Top Manager No. 1. The flip side of their popularity is that their private lives become subject to scrutiny and that they run the risk of their management mistakes being pilloried. Society rides the roller coaster along with them: It first cheers top managers and then attacks them when the opportunity is right. On the one hand, top managers serve both the media as a topic for coverage and ordinary citizens as a projection of their own ideals and desires. On the other, just like everyone else, they are unable to withdraw from the mainstream. This includes generally valid ideas and values, which are accepted by the majority of society during a certain period of time. It is nearly impossible to swim against the tide. Anyone who nevertheless does so has to expect condemnation by society. People normally seek respect and approval from society, not disdain.

It is not only top managers at banks who are exposed to the mainstream but also their clients, regulators, central bankers, economic analysts, and professors. In the years preceding the financial crisis, mainstream in the economy meant, inter alia, belief in the self-regulation of markets, the ability to quantify future risks through computer modeling, and continual progress thanks to stable markets.[96] Ethnical questions, as well as the findings of neurosciences and psychology, were suppressed or dismissed as irrelevant to the financial markets.[97] The employees of governmental bank regulators[98] and central banks believed in this just as much as did analysts at rating agencies and university instructors. A high degree of consensus predominates in a financial system in which the most important actors agree that the same basic conditions and requirements prevail for the optimal functioning of markets. Critics have difficulty reaching an audience. Individuals who opposed the mainstream were scorned as "fools in the corner" or "doctors of doom." In 2005 Raghuram Rajan, chief economist of the International Monetary Fund at the time, argued publicly that modern financial instruments do not make markets more stable. In 2006 Nouriel Roubini prophesied that there was a 70% chance of a recession. And starting in 1999, Harry Markopolos, a financial analyst, repeatedly warned U.S. financial regulators about the dubious business practices of one Bernard Madoff.[99] In retrospect, they were all correct, but at the time they raised their criticisms, they were derided. The mainstream ignored them. Just as Fuld, Ospel, Cayne, FitzPatrick, and Corzine presumably put too little stock in their internal cautioners, public critics were cast as spoilsports by the prevailing mainstream in the financial world. "As long as the music is playing, you've got to get up and dance," i.e., top managers at major banks didn't want to pass up the opportunity to make profits. That was how Chuck Prince, CEO of Citigroup, put it in July 2007 as the financial markets started to falter.[100]

To a great extent, the mainstream was responsible for the fact that bank regulators didn't ask critical enough questions, that rating agencies didn't base their ratings on analyses that were more up-to-date and appropriate to the real market, and that consultants were more on the lookout for fees than for weak points. The height of the mainstream was the takeover of ABN AMRO by RBS: ABN AMRO was being advised by Goldman Sachs, UBS, Morgan Stanley, Lehman Brothers, and Rothschild; while RBS was receiving counsel from, inter alia, Merrill Lynch, Greenhill, Santander, and Fortis. They were apparently all in agreement that this was a deal that could not go sour, and they collected millions for their services. And as long as the music is playing...

On the consequences of increasing social inequality

There is a second trend that has become more and more pronounced over the past 20 years: Inequality. The distance between Wall Street, meaning the bank managers working for global financial companies, and Main Street, meaning the employees in all other economic sectors, has grown steadily. The gap between bankers and normal earners is widening relentlessly. On the one side, the rich and super-rich, who in addition to big salaries are earning disproportional bonuses and can afford everything. On the other, normal workers, who are battling rising prices and have to cut back or take out loans. In 2008, inequality reached the level of 1929, the year the Great Depression began.[101] As is the case today, wages at that time diverged wildly, meaning that the majority who earned less suffered much more from the financial crisis than did the privileged few at the other end of the scale. The consequences of this inequality are that the majority of populaces in Europe and the U.S. are losing confidence in the free markets. There is a risk of political instability and poverty, as well as unequal opportunity with respect to access to medical care and education. Political and economic elites are faced with the question of legitimacy. A growing number of citizens feel that they are being treated unfairly, and they see a lack of solidarity on the part of the elite. The political stability, which is one of the most important factors for economic success and prosperity for many, is increasingly being called into question. Extremist or populist movements, which offer simple solutions to worried citizens, are on the rise, threatening the freest possible flow of people, goods, and services.

The major banks have contributed to inequality.[102] They and their top managers have created widespread disbelief and resentment, not only because they offer often incomprehensible products but also because they represent a privileged class. In fact, this class has mutated into caste, since they apparently need only one another and can be understood only from within, as was expressed by the former CEO of Deutsche Bank, Josef Ackermann, in a 2007 interview:

> When I came to Deutsche Bank, I earned two million marks. If I were to be paid a comparable salary today, I would lose all respect. People would say: He doesn't have any market value. That subsequently prompted us to change the salary structure. But of course, that is spoken from the logic of a world that can't be depicted publicly, and I'm well aware of that.[103]

Several top managers have even collected disproportionate bonuses when their banks incurred losses and had to be bailed out with taxpayer money – the antithesis of normal managers and entrepreneurs, who get paid only when they create products that customers buy, generating profits for the company.

During the boom years, our CEOs received eight-figure salaries. These salaries did not correspond to the added value that they created for the real economy with their financial products. Moreover, these salaries were on average more than 300 times higher than that for an employee in the industrial or services sector.[104] People are willing to accept that those bearing responsibility deserve to earn much more. However, the amounts described above create disbelief, since this dimension is no longer comprehensible and it cannot be credibly explained how one person can create added value to that degree. As a result, the banking world violates – at least in the eyes of a large number of citizens – the principle of fairness.

Thain's bonus of millions after poor business performance by Merrill Lynch and Goodwin's large severance package following the near collapse of RBS have left the broad public with the image of the greedy banker, who is primarily out for his own benefit and surely not for the welfare of his employees or the company. At the same time, the rational manager, *homo oeconomicus*, was reduced to an absurdity.

2.6 The phenomenon of power – habituation and hubris

According to Max Weber, power is the "the probability that one actor within a social relationship will be in a position to carry out his own will despite resistance."[105] Accordingly, power is the energy that moves the social system.[106] Power comes into being within individuals and expresses itself in the way they communicate and behave. The relationship between top managers and the people they lead is a factor that is central to the success of every company. The smoother the power relationships function, the more energy is available to achieve the organization's objectives.[107]

When journalists ask top managers how they wield their power, they usually answer evasively or refer to their responsibility. This is understandable, since power has a bad reputation among the public. The aspiration to exert one's influence is generally equated with the desire to dominate others and to earn a large salary. And yet, power is neither good nor bad. Power cannot be gainsaid or argued away, since it is a part of our social existence. We apply it daily in our relationships with colleagues, friends, and family. And because power only arises in a social context, it is inconceivable that common action is possible without the exercise of power.

Development of power

Power develops from complex interrelationships among an individual's physical attributes, social skills, and neurological predispositions.

Physical aspects, such as appearance, size, vitality, and stamina, are key elements to achieving a position of power. According to one study, more than 90% of CEOs are taller than 5 feet, 7 inches, while another claims that one half of all board chairmen of Fortune 500 companies are taller than 6 feet.[108] An attractive appearance and vitality impart charisma and give the impression of superiority, energy, and stamina: This person seems capable of exercising power positively. But physical attributes alone are not enough. Power cannot be achieved without the will to acquire it, nor without so-called politicizing power strategies.

These include intensive management of relationships and reputation. In organizations, personal networks are indispensable to a career. As one ascends the career ladder, personal relationships become more important, while expertise and the performance associated with it become less significant. Power strategies also include opportunistic conduct. Individuals act opportunistically when, for example, they look primarily to the organization's top managers, seek to be close to them, share their views, and desire to serve them. If power relationships change, they immediately reprioritize. They are less interested in the company and its objectives and values than in gaining an advantage for themselves. Opportunistic individuals generally show relatively low adherence to conventions and moral concepts, little affective participation in interpersonal relationships, and a marked ability to adapt to circumstances facing them.

Battle for power positions

In the battle for power positions, the following neurological prerequisites seem to play a role:

- First, synaptic plasticity: The will to acquire power, along with a pronounced drive for power, influence the corresponding networks in the brain, creating a psychological prerequisite for reinforcing behavioral patterns. "Built-in" behavior is perfected through repeated use.
- Second, mirror neurons: These have to do with nerve cells that, due to consciousness stimuli, activate in an observer's brain the same programs that are running in the brain of an acting person, as though the observer were acting. This is associated with the ability to surmise the reactions of others, i.e., to anticipate them. The more efficiently this network of neurons is developed, the better it appears that an individual will be capable of applying power strategies. It seems that charming, charismatic managers have precisely those abilities.[109]
- Third, a higher level of serotonin, which is a hormone that regulates well-being. Whereas too little serotonin leads to depression, increased serotonin levels trigger a feeling of serenity and equilibrium, thereby engendering positive behavior.

Once a certain power position has been achieved, two behavioral patterns can be discerned: Some managers remain in *climbing mode*. They orient their behavior more toward their direct competitors than toward their employees. The desire for recognition and career appears to cause an addiction-like dependency. Climbing-mode managers also stand to benefit from an organizational culture that is fixated on meritocracy and a willingness to take risks. In an environment such as this, managers with pronounced neurological prerequisites with respect to climbing hierarchies normally have a limited behavior repertoire. Other managers switch to *cruising mode*, though they still keep an eye on higher hierarchical levels. These managers focus most of their attention on their employees and are concerned about creating stable structures. They appear to be particularly endowed with the social skills of self-perception and self-control, as well as with a large behavior repertoire and a broad spectrum of interests and concepts that they can draw upon and flexibly modify to meet the situation.

Power conflicts become a perpetual individual experience. The individual's career is dominated by the opportunity to climb up the ladder and the risk of falling from it, by success or failure in competition with others. Their biography reads like a sequence of power struggles, both voluntary and involuntary, won and lost.[110]

The battle for influential positions is sometimes waged with opportunistic methods and the proverbial elbows. But once the hierarchy is set, the power so achieved contributes to stability and eliminates further conflicts. Trust, which is not one of the features of a power struggle, now becomes an important element in positive collaboration between managers and employees. Although in practice, rituals related to the demonstration or testing of power take place on a daily basis – seating arrangements, speaking orders at meetings, greeting and introduction procedures, rules regarding company cars, parking, and office furniture – clarification of the issue of rank leads to a more harmonious and efficient working environment.

The pay-off for a position in top management consists of elevated status, which is compensated with recognition and a lot of money. The insignia of power consist of, for example, an office in a preferred location on the top floor with new furniture, a company jet, a private chauffeur, etc. The price to be paid for this is assuming broad responsibility for the long-term benefit of stakeholders. While middle and lower management bear various subordinate responsibilities for company areas or projects, they are not accountable for the whole.

Risks of power

What happens to people in power positions?[111] In the following, I will focus on top managers, although we are also aware of executives in middle management and junior managers who have abused their positions of power, who thoroughly terrorize their teams in an authoritarian, egotistical manner, and who desert their colleagues on important projects. In general, these types of behavior result in the end of career advancement. Only rarely do managers make it into top management once they have acquired a bad reputation.

When people have been in powerful positions for a long period, there is a risk of habituation and hubris. Even the top manager's status itself seems to trigger certain disinhibiting behavior. In an experiment conducted at the Stanford School of Business, several groups of four students each were instructed to discuss a political problem. One member of each group was named the boss. Then, a plate of five cookies was brought in, and the bosses unashamedly ate the remaining one. In addition, video recordings showed that the bosses developed bad manners, for example, eating with their mouths open and scattering crumbs. Bosses are also those individuals who often put their feet up on the desk, leave people waiting without reason, interrupt others, make jokes at the expense of others, and feel that they are the only ones who don't have to comply with internal company regulations and rules of behavior, to name just a few examples.[112]

Habituation

When managers have been at the peak of power for years, they are at risk of habituation: They have gotten accustomed to people listening to them and taking everything they say as the gospel truth. The successes they have achieved are the best evidence that their actions have been correct. They feel entitled to make more money than is due, to be influential and privileged. They feel that it is virtually their right to be compensated at customary industry rates on account of their personal commitment and having dedicated their life solely to the company.

One might imagine that Fuld, Cayne, FitzPatrick, and Ospel, all of whom worked their way to the very top thanks to tireless commitment, remained in touch with day-to-day business and ordinary employees. Responsibly minded generals know that while their strategies and plans are very important, all of their efforts would be for naught if their officers and soldiers failed to implement them. The memories of times when generals held a rifle or CEOs brooded about a specific transaction can fade away, particularly when top positions come with status symbols and prestige. With the personal chauffeur, the private limousine, the parking space in the garage, and the elevator reserved just for them, top managers can forget just how much they need their employees, without whom they would never reach their goal.[113]

When the heads of the European banking world got together in the spring of 2009, they also invited bank CEOs who had resigned in the course of the financial crisis. One participant told me that during the meeting, there were repeated, spontaneous "death vigils." Former CEOs and their spouses were said to have complained that their lives had been "taken" from them. It was in this vein that Bob Hayward, CEO of British Petroleum, reacted to the environmental catastrophe in the Gulf of Mexico, when he said in an interview, "I want my life back." What they all meant was the loss of their positions of power and the privileges that go along with their status, like chauffeurs, household servants, and invitations to cultural events. They had become so accustomed to that life that they couldn't imagine a different one.

Hubris

The second risk is hubris. When a top manager has been successful for years, he sees nothing but opportunities, while paying less attention to risks. Everything seems feasible. Hubris results in one losing touch with reality and the capacity for self-criticism, and it leads to ungrounded behavior and actions, surrounded by yes-men.[114] Carl Schmitt spoke in this context of the "stratosphere of power":

> Outside of each room of direct power, there is an anteroom of indirect influences and forces, an access to the ear, a corridor to the soul of the power holder. Without this anteroom and without this corridor, there is no human power. [...]
>
> The corridor cuts the power holder free from the ground and lifts him up into a stratosphere in which he can reach only those who control him indirectly, whereas he can no longer reach all the other people over whom he exercises power, nor can they any longer reach him.[115]

Without the phenomenon of power, the majority of our case studies would be inconceivable. Think of the CEOs – especially Fuld, Ospel, Cayne, Fitz-Patrick, and Groenink – who undoubtedly tolerated only optimists and can-do people in their circle and didn't want to listen to any more critics. In this way, they created the risk of becoming prisoners of their own systems. Only if a top manager has a wealth of power, is detached from reality, and over-estimates himself, can he make a decision, like Thain, to all at once fire a large number of employees, hire new top managers with lucrative contracts, renovate his office at a cost equivalent to the annual salary of ten mid-level employees, and award himself an eight-figure bonus despite poor business results. One can attribute this to the theory of instrumental exercise of power elaborated by Heinrich Popitz: A yes-no formula is introduced. If you question the power of CEOs like Fuld or Goodwin with a no, then you have to question your own position in the organization. You have challenged the alpha male and must now risk being driven from the pack.

The case of Jamie Dimon and the loss of billions in 2012 appears to me to be one of double hubris: First, his increasingly uncritical attitude about his double role as board chairman and CEO, and second, his over-estimation of the autonomy, critical judgment, and openness of his top managers.

Cases of tragic hubris by top managers are not limited to the banking world alone. Hans-Rudolf Merz, former Swiss Minister of Finance and at the time President of the Swiss Confederation, travelled personally and without the agreement of his government colleagues to meet with the Libyan despot Gaddafi in order to free two hostages. He returned empty-handed. Perhaps he was influenced by an earlier positive experience: In 1968, after Soviet troops invaded Czechoslovakia in response to the Prague Spring, he travelled by car to Prague to pick up a student friend from the occupied city. Another example involves Professor Turina, a world-renowned heart surgeon, and his medical team from the Zurich University Hospital. After dozens of successful open-heart surgeries, they allowed themselves to be persuaded to transplant a new heart into a patient in front of live television cameras. The patient died, because the blood type of the new heart didn't match hers. The reasons that led to the patient receiving such a donor heart are unresolved. Could it possibly be that due to their experience and successes, the physicians on Professor Turina's team felt too assured and neglected certain controls and arrangements?[116]

2.7 Situation and chance – double incomprehension and new illusions

Every situation is unique, requiring a distinct decision. This doesn't mean that we make a conscious decision in every instance. This would overtax our brains – decisions are made on the basis of routine and experience. On the one hand, this constitutes a special strength, which enables us to undertake certain daily actions automatically while we're occupied thinking about other things. On the other, it is associated with certain weaknesses, since the brain connects each new situation with patterns and models, thus influencing the decision-making process. This means that while we are not pre-determined, we are at least conditioned. Our options and thus our decisions are steered down a certain track. If a decision in the past proved to be correct, it should also lead to a reasonable choice in this situation. However, this natural decision-making process[117] can mislead us, since situations may resemble one another but are not identical. A good decision in the past may be a wrong one today, since circumstances may have changed or other individuals may be involved. Even small changes create a new constellation in which individual factors come into contact with one another. In turn, these interrelationships themselves create new constellations. In the process, a meaningful role is also played by chance, i.e., that which was unforeseeable or could not be anticipated through human assessment. We then interpret chance – depending on the point of view – as a beneficial factor or not.

History does not repeat itself

The uniqueness of every situation is well illustrated by an example passed down from Lie Yukou:

> In the Lu Province there lived a scholar named Xi, who had two sons. One loved scholarship, the other weaponry. One of them approached the ruler of Ji, who appointed him the tutor of all princes. The other went to Xu, where the king promoted him to general. The income of the two brothers made Xi's whole family rich.
>
> Xi had a neighbor named Meng, who likewise had two sons who had the same professions. However, Meng's family was beset by poverty. Meng turned to Xi's family and asked for advice. The two sons told him about how everything really happened. Meng's sons then approached the rulers and offered them their services. But neither son was successful, and both suffered harm to body and soul.
>
> Meng went to Xi to complain, and the latter answered as follows: "He who comes in time will succeed; he who comes too late will end in ruin. Your family's path was the same as ours, but the outcome was different. This is because you were not in time, not because you were lacking in your actions. Moreover, in the world there is no truth that would be correct in every circumstance, nor any action that would be incorrect in every circumstance. That which was needed in the past is perhaps cast off today. That which is cast off today will perhaps

be needed at a later point. Whether something is needed or unneeded – this does not follow a hard and fast rule. How one uses an opportunity, does so in time, adjusts oneself to circumstances – there is no formula for this. Everything depends on prudence. Without this prudence, even a man as scholarly as Kung Kiu and as able Lu Shang could go forth and surely fail to succeed." Father Meng and his sons were satisfied with this answer.[118]

Thus, according to Master Yukou, an individual can be termed prudent if he adjusts himself to a certain situation, finds the right moment, and then makes the suitable decision.

In his *Discourses*, Niccolo Machiavelli remarked as follows about adjusting to situations:

I have often reflected that the causes of the success or failure of men depend upon their manner of suiting their conduct to the times. We see one man proceed in his actions with passion and impetuosity; and as in both the one and the other case men are apt to exceed the proper limits, not being able always to observe the just middle course, they are apt to err in both. But he errs least and will be most favored by fortune who suits his proceedings to the times, as I have said above, and always follows the impulses of his nature. [...] It is this which assures to republics greater vitality and more enduring success than monarchies have; for the diversity of the genius of her citizens enables the republic better to accommodate herself to the changes of the times than can be done by a prince. For any man accustomed to a certain mode of proceeding will never change it, as we have said, and consequently when time and circumstances change, so that his ways are no longer in harmony with them, he must of necessity succumb.[119]

In the biography of his ancestor the Duke of Marlborough, one of the greatest military commanders, Winston S. Churchill wrote:

But no battle ever repeats itself. The success of a commander does not arise from following rules or models. It consists in an absolutely new comprehension of the dominant facts of the situation at the time, and all the forces at work. Cooks use recipes for dishes and doctors have prescriptions for diseases, but every operation of war is unique.[120]

By studying history, generals and politicians should become aware of the uniqueness of situations and the limited applicability of military and political experiences. However, history is full of examples of how commanders and ministers prepared for an earlier war and were insufficiently capable of including the social and technological changes since the previous war into their strategies. One recalls, for example, the Maginot Line, which was a response to France's high death toll in the First World War but offered no protection against mobile warfare dominated by tanks and planes, which would come to define tactics in the Second World War.

We all cherish routine and avoid change

But a given situation never remains constant. The clock is always ticking. Once there is a change in circumstances – whether these are intrinsic to the involved individuals themselves or have to do with outside factors – a new situation arises, which in turn presents different problems and challenges. It is impossible to predict with certainty how quickly this might occur. In some cases, a single event is enough to create a completely new situation literally overnight, such as an accident or catastrophe that turns everything on its head. In other cases, change slowly insinuates itself into situations, as on a project team that is working together over many months. It may be that the involved individuals barely notice the changes as they are taking place. It is not until sales figures start to fall or customer complaints begin to mount that the team wakes up or comes under sharp criticism from project managers. Consumers change their habits, and both markets and stock prices experience changes. Why is it that we so often fail to recognize this until it is too late? Why is it that we refuse to acknowledge the law of changing situations?

We are creatures of habit and resist any attempt at change. We are comfortable in our routine and always seek out the familiar. Scientists have invented a sort of magic spell designed to protect them against change of any kind. They often say *ceteribus paribus*, "Under the assumption that nothing changes..." or "All other things being held constant..." But reality is of course blind to such caveats. There is no such thing as a model scenario or a prescription that would be applicable to all situations and events or that could be used to predict future market developments.[121]

We are clearly loath to reassess matters. This might be what happened to Fuld, Ospel, FitzPatrick, and Corzine: They tackled the problems of today using the experiences and successes of yesterday. In so doing, they didn't recognize – or perhaps refused to believe – that innovative financial products and new actors had emerged in an increasingly overheated market.

New situation, new boss?

The individual charged with formal responsibility has to be capable of making the right decision in every situation. Otherwise, he or she has to make way for someone else. A plane crash that occurred in the Andes is a particularly illustrative example of the impact that a change of leadership can have. On October 13, 1972, 45 people from Mendoza, Uruguay, were taking a flight over the Andes, heading toward Santiago de Chile. On board were the members of the Old Christians rugby team, accompanied by family members, friends, and fans, as well as four crew members. Their plane crashed in a remote region of the Argentinian Andes, bursting into pieces as it came to rest on a glacier at an elevation of 3,600 meters. Twenty-seven people initially survived the crash. During the night of October 30, an avalanche buried the fuselage, which the survivors were using for shelter, costing the lives of eight more people. Others subsequently died of malnutrition, exhaustion, or their injuries. Ultimately, two survivors set out on a 10-day trek across the Andes to get help, and on December 22, the 15 survivors were rescued.[122]

As captain of the rugby team, Marcelo Perez was the formal leader. Directly following the crash and in the days thereafter, he proved to be an exemplary manager. However, the circumstances changed dramatically following the radio report that the search was being called off for the plane that had been lost in the Andes. Having firmly believed that they would be rescued within days, Marcelo was unable to handle this new situation. It overwhelmed him and caused him to fall into a deep depression, which turned him into a follower instead of a leader.

This brought about a new situation in which a fresh leader emerged: One who had not lost hope of a rescue, who no longer waited for it passively but instead searched actively for solutions. Gustavo Zerbino put together a small expedition team that, under his leadership, was to search for the remaining parts of the wreckage with the aim of finding, in addition to articles of clothing and food, the radio and making contact with the outside world. In addition, he hoped to be able to see across the mountains in order to estimate the chances for an expedition to look for help. This venture nearly ended in catastrophe. The weather conditions in the Andes and the physical strain led to exhaustion, from which Gustavo and his companions were slowly able to recover only with effort. His leadership potential was exhausted.

As a result, a new situation once again emerged: Adding to the fact that the search for survivors had been called off, there was the experience of the physical and psychological strain of an expedition in the high mountains. Now the focus was first on ensuring their very survival and then slowly gaining strength to make it possible for a few of the party to look for help. Most of the survivors were convinced that this was a realistic strategy. In this situation, they didn't need direct leadership by an individual but rather a strong community. Carried by mutual hope and based on the above strategy, they broke up into teams that had got along well prior to the catastrophe due to common interests and concerns. In this regard, Fito Strauch's team played a particularly cohesive role. During this phase, strong personalities, like Roberto Canessa, had room to develop. Roberto, an independent, creative, but stubborn medical student, gave the survivors important impulses with his initiatives. Among other things, he convinced them that there was only one chance of survival: They would have to bring themselves to eat the flesh of the dead. In addition, he spent days trying to repair the radio, but he was ultimately unsuccessful. However, Roberto was too much of a lone wolf and did too little to integrate with the group to be recognized by everyone as their leader.

During the weeks following an avalanche, the hopes of the survivors focused on Nando Parrado. Even in the early stages of the fight for survival, he seemed inspired by the idea of looking for help. Thanks to the growing awareness that if they didn't want to die, the group would have to be rescued in the next few weeks, and thanks to the experiences gained from several short expeditions, Nando Parrado and Roberto Canessa ultimately set out. Compared to their companions, the two were in the best physical and psychological shape to take the risk. During the ten-day tour de force, Nando was the leader and dictated the path and the speed. Roberto was the critical force, though following the same objective and optimally complementing the informal leader.

Not every person is suited to every situation. Some people adjust, while others give up, which doesn't mean that they failed and no longer have a future as leaders. Only those who quit completely and resist their fate will no longer be able to pick themselves up. Falling down is possible, maybe even healthy for junior managers, because it teaches them something. But the important thing is to get back up and confront new situations and thus new opportunities. However, as the case of the survivors in the Andes shows, one sometimes just lacks the energy for this, or one is simply not up for it.

Because of the inhumanely harsh conditions in the Andes, the change of leadership came about naturally. In normal economic life, the situation is of course different. Changes at the top of an organization happen because the top manager either resigns or is fired. In most cases, when top managers can't handle a changed situation or the company loses faith in their abilities, the parties agree to go their separate ways.

In democracies, leaders are turned out of office when voters believe a change is called for. Churchill was an outstanding prime minister during wartime, but the British were less confident that he could lead the country through the postwar years and failed to reelect him shortly after the end of the Second World War. George H.W. Bush was successful against the Iraqi dictator Saddam Hussein after the latter invaded Kuwait, but despite his military and foreign-policy successes, the American electorate denied Bush a second term because it believed him to be less capable of stimulating the economy in his own country.

Obviously, the top managers in our case studies brought successes to their banks. For this, they were celebrated, sometimes even honored with awards and knighthoods. These successes were attributed to them. Since their management boards and administrative boards were in lockstep with them, they likely neglected to periodically analyze social and economic developments. They neither demanded that top management review the current state of affairs, nor did they do so themselves. They also failed to question whether the CEO's successes were attributable to the overall context of favorable constellations or perhaps merely to coincidence.

Chance plays a role

It is difficult for us to admit that there is no discernible cause for the occurrence of a certain event or that it objectively happens without cause. Perhaps we know a few factors that influenced it, but we can't measure or control them. In economic and financial matters, we believe that a result occurred solely because of our decisions and actions. However, we fail to recognize that we have no precise understanding of either the actions of our competitors or the purchasing behavior of customers. Moreover, there are many other factors – such as weather, logistics, and the political environment – that can work to shape the end result. As Stefan Klein observed,[123] it is conceivable that there is no such thing as chance but merely a great number of undefined factors that we can't influence or measure. With roulette, the number on which the ball lands depend on, inter alia, the surface of the ball, air temperature or draft, and the croupier's hand movements. But the fact remains that the end result is unpredictable.

On the one hand, we are baffled by the phenomenon of chance, tending to deny its validity. On the other, we fall victim to errors in judgment. In *The Gambler*, Fyodor Dostoyevsky's protagonist mused as follows:

> It seemed to me that calculation was superfluous, and by no means possessed of the importance which certain other players attached to it, even though they sat with ruled papers in their hands, whereon they set down the coups, calculated the chances, reckoned, staked, and – lost exactly as we more simple mortals did who played without any reckoning at all. However, I deduced from the scene one conclusion which seemed to me reliable – namely, that in the flow of fortuitous chances there is, if not a system, at all events a sort of order. This, of course, is a very strange thing. For instance, after a dozen middle figures there would always occur a dozen or so outer ones. Suppose the ball stopped twice at a dozen outer figures; it would then pass to a dozen of the first ones, and then, again, to a dozen of the middle ciphers, and fall upon them three or four times, and then revert to a dozen outers; whence, after another couple of rounds, the ball would again pass to the first figures, strike upon them once, and then return thrice to the middle series – continuing thus for an hour and a half, or two hours. One, three, two: one, three, two. It was all very curious. Again, for the whole of a day or a morning the red would alternate with the black, but almost without any order, and from moment to moment, so that scarcely two consecutive rounds would end upon either the one or the other. Yet, next day, or, perhaps, the next evening, the red alone would turn up, and attain a run of over two score, and continue so for quite a length of time – say, for a whole day.[124]

The halo effect can mislead us into trusting the first impression, or, like the gambler, we believe that we discover a pattern in a certain chain of events. But much of this is attributable only to chance or to the dimension of the apparently inexplicable.

Experienced traders and computer models –
the illusion of calculability

Terry Odean studied 163,000 stock transactions over a period of seven years. He came to the conclusion that those traders who maintained that they knew which stocks to buy or sell based on their analyses or experiences did not on average generate higher profits than normal investors who acted as they saw fit. The subjective experience and knowledge of traders do of course lead to objectively comprehensible decisions. But in situations of uncertainty and complexity, these decisions begin to resemble a blind choice. Trading in financial products is therefore comparable to gambling.[125]

Information technology has made it possible to simulate the reality of the financial economy using computer models. The aptly named Monte Carlo simulation is used in order to depict future trends. The model is capable of simulating a number of scenarios simultaneously and making predictions within seconds, for example, with respect to risks. Bankers and financial experts believed that this made it possible to predict and control the future. The financial crisis proved that which few had challenged: that computer models in fact contain only assumptions, which may be unilateral or even wrong, and they can never depict total complexity or predict future events.[126] The real (financial) economy is complex, and it is influenced by a number of factors that affect a given situation. For this reason, it is not possible for us to rely either on subjective impressions and perceptions or on data based on computer models. Mathematical models and computer simulations are no substitute for human cooperation in the sense of networked, critical thinking and evaluation.[127] They are useful as aids for decision-makers, but not as oracles.[128]

We fail to comprehend the law of changing situations and the likelihood that chance will occur, since the exact time and the particulars of their appearance are not predictable. And because we think that there are patterns or models with which we can control them, we fall for an illusion.

2.8 Conflicting Challenges

The foregoing remarks have shown that we tend to conform our behavior and not to attract attention by taking contrary positions, particularly when everyone else is of the same opinion. Teams, like management committees, management boards, and supervisory boards, as well as political bodies, display a tendency toward groupthink, and entire systems feel the herd instinct. Obedience, groupthink, herd instinct, and mainstream are various forms of conformity.

The greater the success achieved, the more entrenched top managers become and the more pronounced their self-confidence. This raises the pressure to conform on their directly subordinate managers and their closest assistants. The connection between conformity and errors in reasoning results in top managers adopting an out-of-touch, autocratic management style and in the loss of reality, diversity of opinion, alternatives, and risk controls.

It might be that the top managers in our case studies fell victim to a number of mistakes, illusions, preconceptions, and errors in reasoning, which led them to make bad decisions. I call these "irrational," if they were made under strong emotions and against better judgment.

I've also noticed that the financial industry seems to have been smitten by a deceptive harmony. A self-referential system caused top management, banks, governmental oversight authorities, rating agencies, consulting firms, and academia to all be in lockstep: The same objectives (profit, reputation, economic prosperity), the same models and methods, and similar milieus and cultures led to homogeneous political and financial beliefs and, ultimately, to a collective boom and crash.

In the following, I describe a number of aspects of irrationality from which top managers may suffer.

Egomania

We are all egotists and have an "ego gene." We wish to survive, and many of us strive to achieve the highest possible status in the group. Ambition is not equivalent to egotism, let alone egomania. Without a dose of ambition, one doesn't become the boss. Professional advancement and entrepreneurial success are virtually inconceivable without ambitious people. But when top managers start to behave narcissistically, i.e., when they become completely out of balance (between orientation toward performance and toward employees) and think only about themselves and their success and have no sensitivity whatsoever for others or for social groups, ambition becomes counterproductive and damaging for the entire firm.

Top managers are egomaniacs when absolutely everything revolves around them and their pathological urge for recognition, prestige, and status, and when everything else is made subordinate to these objectives. Egomaniacs don't speak and act the same way. They talk about *their* employees and *their* shareholders, for whose welfare they feel responsible. They propagate this at in-house events, public speaking engagements, and to the media. Who would say anything different in public? But their actions betray them. Their personal status and advantage are the focus of their efforts, not the longer-term welfare of the firm and its employees, shareholders, and customers. Egomaniacs give no thought to the fact that they, too, are merely employees of the firm and are replaceable.

I see egomaniacal traits in at least a few protagonists. For them, the focus is on status and prestige within the company, the financial sector, or society. With Kerviel, Ospel, FitzPatrick, Goodwin, and Corzine, perceived humbler origins or education might have been the main driver of their desire for recognition. In at least one case (Dreier), envy of higher earners seems to have motivated fraudulent actions. With others (Malde, Thain, Groenink, Goodwin), I sense that they were compelled by a mania to compete and to be better than the rest. What I also find noteworthy is the connection between egomaniacal traits, testosterone (street fighter culture, macho behavior), and certain types of sports and games (hunting, golf, bridge), particularly with Cayne, Fuld, Groenink, and Goodwin.

Compensation

In all of our case studies, the individuals earned a lot of money. This was especially the case for the top managers. Money – wages in compensation of worked performed, as well as bonuses as additional remuneration for extraordinary services in the case of company success – embodies professional success and is a boon to achieving a higher social status. Top managers think and convince themselves that they have honestly earned it through above-average efforts, and they point to their competitors, whose compensation is the same or even higher. Hardly anyone denies their personal engagement and the stress associated with the job. However, they aren't the only ones who work hard. And without their employees, they could in no way deliver the same performance.

Money has a "rational–irrational, vulgar–divine double character."[129] On the one hand, money is a strong motivator[130] – when we're paid more, we feel good and believe that our performance has been judged positively. This is why companies pay bonuses. In my experience, about 70% of employees at major banks leave their companies because a competitor has offered them more money. Money can buy happiness in a certain sense, and it affirms to us as individuals that our commitment is being rewarded. On the other hand, money does not make us more social or empathetic. Just the opposite! It targets our ego. We are satisfied with ourselves and are anxious to continue to work loyally for the company in order to be correspondingly compensated with money. Studies have shown that the prospect of money makes people more egotistical and lowers social responsibility toward others,[131] making them less willing to help others and to work with them. Likewise, money appears to neutralize critical thinking. When we take care of people, we're not thinking about money. But if we are overly preoccupied with making money, then empathy dwindles, as does the willingness to try to understand people and their feelings. We can see this phenomenon especially with Thain, who undertook expensive recruitments and office renovations while at the same time firing hundreds of employees and instituting rigorous cost-cutting measures. I see an attempt to moderate pecuniary egotism in the charity efforts of FitzPatrick and Groenink, as well as in the purchase of artwork (Dreier).

Eroticism

At least with Goodwin and Corzine, eroticism played a certain role. Erotic relationships, as well as casual sex on business trips or simply when the opportunity arose, have proved to be the undoing for not a few top managers.

This should essentially come as no surprise, since eroticism is one of our basic feelings and drives. It brings pleasure, invigorates our lives, stimulates our senses, and allows us to consciously experience a basic human need, namely, physical desire. The world is full of eroticism and, at least in a certain sense, also full of temptations. Many people, especially attractive women, have erotic capital.[132]

As with every other person, top managers are exposed to this minefield. Eroticism can give them energy or cloud their senses. They are at the top in the hierarchy of a group, a company. The higher up they are, the greater the opportunity for erotic adventures. Power is attractive and tempting. In a survey of 1,250 managers in the Netherlands, 329 of them, or 26.3%, indicated that they had had extra-marital relationships. Apparently, there were no significant differences between male and female managers.[133]

Top managers wield influence, are a topic of media interest, and for this very reason act like a magnet to other people. Their status is admired. Their dominance and power have an erotic effect, their money, an attractive one. This is why we see so many beautiful women at the side of much older top managers; although these women leave them when the managers lose their social status, position of power, wealth, or everything altogether.

Eroticism becomes a trap that ensnares top managers. It also brings about their fall when they make decisions that are not in the interest and for the benefit of the company but rather provide nothing more than personal satisfaction or create an unjustified advantage for the object of their desire. Fred Goodwin and Jon Corzine are by far not the only prominent top managers who got into trouble due to their erotic attractiveness. Top managers from politics and industry have had to reckon with grievous consequences: Eliot Spitzer, the highly principled governor of New York, had to resign due to his liaisons with prostitutes.[134] Paul Wolfowitz, who as president of the World Bank arranged for his girlfriend to receive bonuses and promotions,[135] lost his job, as did Dominique Strauss-Kahn, former president of the International Monetary Fund, who allegedly had sex with a hotel maid. Top managers at Siemens, who went on trips with prostitutes at the company's expense, were fired and criminally prosecuted. A subsidiary of the insurance group Munich Re rewarded its sales managers with a trip to a wellness spa in Budapest. What made this spa special was that dozens of prostitutes were available, who were identified with various armbands. Women with white armbands were reserved for directors and the most successful managers.[136]

Prestige and power can mislead people into creating advantages for themselves at the expense of others. It is no surprise that this becomes a feeding frenzy for the media, which report extensively about these affairs and liaisons. This stigmatizes top managers in the eyes of the public and destabilizes them in their position of power and as the standard bearers for their companies.

Exhaustion

Top managers are constantly at work, always on the go, reachable by phone 24 hours a day. They have a full agenda. They are on call at all times, including on weekends and while on vacation, and arrange for teleconferences when their wives and children purportedly have other plans. Our

CEOs are no exception to this. They are baby boomers, who are known to be workaholics.

Positions of power and the related positive energy that comes from recognition and esteem are good for their health.[137] We can find confirmation of this in the fact that when powerful politicians and economic leaders finish their careers, they tend to become ill. They stay hale and hearty as long as they feel that they are irreplaceable and valued. But once they retire or are out of the public spotlight, they have to deal with disabilities or serious illnesses. The list is a long one, ranging from toppled power holders, like the Shah of Iran or presidents Milošević and Mubarak, to politicians who have been voted out of office or reached the end of their term, like Helmut Kohl and François Mitterrand.

There are top managers who in their very limited free time seek additional challenges and confirmation. They participate in marathons or climb the peaks of the tallest mountains, physically demanding activities that require months of training and mental conditioning. In addition to work-related stress, they subject their bodies to further strain. While that may be well and good, in that it brings top managers additional satisfaction and confirmation, it can also overwhelm the body and mind and lead to exhaustion or increased stress and thus be a recipe for bad decision making.

Top managers who seek their daily kick from long hours are ill aware of the fact they may become exhausted over time, overtax their bodies, and start to act like drunks – which is why they are called workaholics, a word made of up "work" and "alcoholic." In this condition, they are emotionally unstable, have limited perception, are open only to their inner circle, and are thus at risk of making bad decisions.

Experiences

Top managers have a wealth of professional and personal experiences. This wealth means that they immediately have their own opinions about every issue and every task that arises in areas that they are familiar with. The opinion, idea, or impression is simply there. It comes from their individual wealth of experience that they have accumulated over the course of their lives. That is certainly a positive thing, because in this way, they quickly have plausible, competent responses to many problems in their familiar environment, responses that can be readily realized and thereby exude a sense of confidence.

The experiences of top managers have negative aspects when they stop listening, know everything better from the outset, and thwart every emerging dialogue at its inception; when they prevent others from speaking with them, presenting contrary ideas, or even simply reporting bad news; or when they no longer verify their own intuitive opinion by collecting facts and seeking the views of other experienced people and thus make rash decisions.

In our examples, we can probably discern the power of prior experiences with Thain, Ospel, Groenink, Goodwin, and Corzine. In investment banking, they experienced practiced meritocracy and saw it as a future cash machine for themselves and their company, whereby they must have viewed traditional banking, with its lengthy decision-making processes and complicated customer relationships, as boring and not very profitable. Having been on top for a long period of time, and with their personal experience of having mastered all problems and crises, Fuld and Cayne probably became convinced that they could manage every difficult situation. Fuld was certainly marked by the power struggles that led to the loss of independence and sale of Lehman Brothers to the extent that he gathered only those around him who were loyal. Furthermore he no longer tolerated criticism, whether of an institutional or individual nature.

Experiences can have extreme effects even with junior managers. With Malde, his experiences in high society (parties, beautiful girls, travel) in his short life may have led to such an entrenched notion of a fulfilled existence that he could not imagine any other. Kerviel likely recognized early on at the bank that high profits brought esteem and recognition from his colleagues, regardless of the manner in which they were made.

Emotions

We are born with emotions. Without emotions, we would hardly be able to survive. Without emotions, we would be incapable of making decisions. Every experience has an emotional marker, a label, that is stamped with, for example, "delight," "in happy expectation," or "I'm sad," "I'm angry." Emotions are a part of our social existence, enabling us to be a part of a group, an organization, a society.

Emotions are reflected in our facial expressions, our demeanor, and our behavior. Babies can read the emotions of their mothers on their faces: When a mother smiles at her baby, the baby smiles back. In general, we are more adept at recognizing negative emotions. When someone is sad, we feel sympathy; when someone is angry, we are wary. While delight may be contagious, it is something that's easier to hide than fear, panic, or disgust.

We are reminded at this juncture of the quick-tempered nature and macho behavior of Fuld, Goodwin, and Groenink. In my view, Malde showed signs of fear of failure, and Dreier, Kerviel, and Ospel likely suffered from feelings of inferiority. A certain degree of arrogance may have played a role with Thain, Cayne, and Corzine. In addition, I suspect that several top managers had an aversion to people who either appeared incompetent or were able to keep their positions based primarily on their social origins or educational background. It seems to me that this aversion was especially pronounced with Ospel, Groenink, and Goodwin.

It is unproblematic when top managers are thrilled about a successful deal, unless they attribute all of the success to themselves. It becomes problematic when top managers display their negative emotions, which Fuld and Goodwin apparently repeatedly did in dealing with their employees and consultants. It seems that top managers behave this way all too often, as is shown by the following story, which I personally experienced:

> I ran into her by chance at the London City Airport in one of the back corners of the concourse. We sat across from each other, nodded briefly, and then turned to our work. I assumed that she, like I, was stranded here, since a number of flights had been cancelled. No problem for me. There's always plenty to read. Engrossed in my notes, I suddenly heard sobbing. I looked up and saw that she was crying, holding her BlackBerry in her hand. I hesitated for a moment, then spoke to her: "Pardon me, I'm sorry to see you crying. Is there anything I can do for you?" She, too, hesitated a moment, then said, "Yes, could you get me a glass of water? I'll be fine then." So we got to talking. Without being prompted, she began telling me about what had upset her. She showed me the message that she had just received from her boss on her BlackBerry. It read, "Bi..., why is it impossible for you ever to do anything right? You know that I always want a Mercedes. Why can't you reserve the right rental car? F... Y..." I asked, "Does he always speak with you that way? Why do you accept it?" "I know, but I worry about my job in this economy," she said. "He can be nice, too, but lately he's just been shouting at everybody. You know, he had 15 applicants for the job, and he picked me." By the time her flight was called, she had calmed down. "Thank you," she said, and made her way to the gate.

When top managers put their frustration on display or act like alpha males, they initiate a destructive spiral: Employees avoid them, withdraw, stop thinking about the good of the company, overlook risks, call in sick, or look for alternatives. Some managers become infected by the negative behavior of top managers and start to act the same way: They move aggressively against rivals, foment intrigues, or promote silo thinking. Negative emotions and corresponding behavior cripple the motivation of many employees and poison the organization's culture. Every explosion of a manager's negative emotions is bad for the work environment, and the higher up on the hierarchy that this occurs, the more devastating the consequences for the company culture.

Empathy

No one seriously expects that the market or the financial industry should be obligated to comply with a certain moral code. But we have been misguided in putting our faith in *homo oeconomicus* as the driving force for an industry in which the interests of all must be provided for in an ideal manner. Values like fairness, solidarity, and social responsibility were considered to be antithetical to liberty, since it was claimed that the rationality of the individual on the free market – in interplay with the "invisible hand" of the market (Adam Smith) – was sufficient to promote the common good. This view, along with the concept of shareholder value, has turned out to be wrong, and is no longer suitable as a model for our financial system. In one way or another, every action emanating from the (financial) economy influences other parts of the overall economy, the state, and society. In this complex world, nothing is without repercussions.

In fact, the welfare of society depends on several criteria. Surveys have shown that happiness is found not in the richest countries but instead in those in which trust between citizens is greatest.[138]

Inequality, which has sharply increased in the Western world in recent years, poses a threat to the trust between citizens and top management in politics and industry. The fact that top management in the financial industry has willingly accepted it, and has even fueled it and in some cases still does, shows that these powerful figures lack empathy. People without any sense of empathy are psychopaths, who have an extremely negative impact on the world around them.[139]

In general, top managers should not be characterized as psychopaths, nor must they be moral authorities. However, persons in power who are compensated with top salaries have to be expected to be capable, at least in part, of understanding the feelings of others and comporting themselves accordingly.

> When the volcano in Iceland erupted in the spring of 2010 resulting in the near shutdown of international air travel for several days throughout the world, a top manager of Deutsche Bank was in Singapore. He ordered the bank's security department to arrange his travel back to London through a circuitous itinerary. Until he reached Marseille, everything went smoothly. But upon his arriving there, it turned out that all high-speed trains to Paris were fully booked for the next 24 hours. So he summarily ordered the head of security to arrange for an additional railcar to be added …

Thain's renovation of his office for more than USD 1 million, the dubious financial dealings of FitzPatrick and Corzine, the excessive bonuses in the face of the impending bankruptcy of their companies in the case of Thain and Goodwin, and the extremely high severance package received by Ospel show a lack of empathy toward citizens, indeed, toward those very same citizens who as customers deposited their savings with them and took out loans, thus contributing to their wealth. As a second invisible hand, empathy constitutes a needed corrective to the invisible hand of the market.

One-dimensionality

The pursuit of profits, better earnings, and performance is important in order for companies to improve their positions against competitors, create new products, gain customers, and ensure jobs. Profits are one-dimensional when they serve only one purpose: to make *me* rich. It is irrelevant how profits are generated, as long as they make the company, and thus me, richer and more prestigious. However, profits have to be pursued within the constraints of laws and contracts, as well as for the benefit of people and organizations. I find this orientation toward society, also with respect to a company's responsibility to state and society, to be lacking with most of the top managers we analyzed, particularly Thain, Fuld, Ospel, Cayne, Groenink, Goodwin, and Corzine.

A company's management acts one-dimensionally when it commits itself to one specific strategy and ignores a holistic approach. This is the case where, within a four-year period, it seeks to be "the best of all investment banks" (Marcel Ospel), targeting all of its efforts solely at competitors instead of at the market as a whole and the implications for society, and treating risk management as a secondary concern. And where management moreover creates two competing investment banks that draw from the same pool of bank money and operate on the same market, the one-dimensionality of strategic action becomes tangible.

One-dimensionality may consist of a group boss focusing on quarterly results or acquisitions while at the same time ignoring operational management and coordination (Groenink, Goodwin) or giving loans exclusively to a small circle of real estate investors (FitzPatrick).

One-dimensionality may consist of the consolidation of power, when top managers have been lodged at top of their companies for years without any limitation on their term of office. Fuld determined the fate of his bank for 14 years, Cayne, for 15 years, and Fitzpatrick, for as long as 22 years. During these years, they created an aura, as well as a power base not unlike a fortress: It is virtually impossible to conquer it with normal means; only an economic crisis can topple it.

Ospel had been CEO since 1997 and group head since 2001. As is the case with Fuld, Cayne, FitzPatrick, Groenink, Goodwin, and Dimon, it becomes evident with Ospel how over time he loaded the management and supervisory board with his minions and out-maneuvered critics. This permitted decisions to be made more swiftly. However, as the crisis emerged, there was no one around to exercise serious oversight, insist on reviewing certain events, criticize certain practices, or warn about impending dangers. Without this counterweight, top managers were left without a holistic view during the decisive phase starting in 2006 and, in the case of Dimon, April 2012. They gave themselves over to the tunnel vision of their own experiences and increasingly distanced themselves from the real economy.

A company's corporate governance is one-dimensional when the chairman of the board and the CEO are one and the same person, as is the case with Jamie Dimon at JP Morgan Chase.

Risk management also has a one-dimensional character when it is lodged in the individual business areas (as was apparently the case at UBS under Ospel and at Lehman Brothers under Fuld) rather than being developed as a holistic instrument (as took place at Deutsche Bank from 2006 to late May 2012) with a chief risk officer who has only this one job and is a member of the management committee or the board. Risk management adequately addresses the complexity of the market only when it relies not merely on rating agencies and empirical data but also brings together all areas that are relevant to risk, takes into consideration trends and highly unlikely events (so-called black swans), and carefully balances the resulting options.

A company culture is one-dimensional when it is based on action dictated from above (Fuld, Cayne, Groenink, Goodwin) and makes streetfighter, macho mentality the standard for internal collaboration. This culture promotes individual achievement, cohesive behavior, and willingness to take risks, while at the same time stifling criticism and cooperation, particularly the removal of silos between areas.

The management or supervisory board acts one-dimensionally when, as with JP Morgan Chase, it relies too heavily on a charismatic top manager and neglects to plan for successors.

Decisions are one-dimensional when they are based solely on computer simulations and mathematical modeling.

Company management acts one-dimensionally when it fails to proactively ready itself for crisis-like circumstances.

Successes

Successes bring pleasure and make people confident, spurring them to further action. No one should begrudge them. They confirm decisions made in the past and reinforce the top manager's claim to leadership. But successes can also promote tunnel vision in top managers, lead them to become blind or arrogant, particularly when they rest on their laurels, or cause them to look for tomorrow's solutions on the basis of yesterday.

Where top managers have been able to celebrate successes over a long period, for example, because of annually rising profits and being named CEO of the Year (Fuld, Groenink, Goodwin), where for years they have been a highly reputed industry leader in their own countries (Ospel, Fitz-Patrick), or where they have done a very good job, at least from a subjective view, of managing many crises and difficulties (Thain, Cayne, Corzine), there is a risk of making decisions about a new situation based on old patterns, as in "If it's not broke, don't fix it." Success first turns into stagnation, then into decline. Top managers are personally convinced that they are capable of mastering all challenges. They stop listening to other voices, disregard warning signs, or suppress indications of trouble. The aura of invincibility and infallibility cloaks them like a protective shield, but in a negative sense, since they are no longer open to other views and options. The people close to them, as well as the managers reporting to them, are likewise convinced of the prolonged wave of success and thus that their boss is making the right decisions. They distance themselves from alternative ideas, prevent contrarians from gaining access to Olympus, and in this way turn themselves into agents.

Agents

In addition to having their directly subordinate top managers, CEOs can also draw on a pool of personal assistants. Thanks to their proximity to the boss, these individuals doubtlessly act also as advisors on all conceivable issues. As a consequence, they exercise considerable influence. It is not without reason that in many cases, the path to the bosses leads over an assistant, who, while loyal to them, is also pursuing his or her own agenda, i.e., his or her own career.

Within the framework of a company's corporate governance, oversight bodies are of particular significance. It goes without saying that the duties of these bodies, which are mandated by law, are important. Despite some differences from country to country in the weight given to them, these obligations also promote competitiveness and thus the company's survival. Just as important as the regulatory rules is the choice of the members of these bodies. If the CEO or group head specifically places only loyal followers, minions, and yes-men in their circle and on supervisory boards – as was evidently done by Fuld, Ospel, Cayne, FitzPatrick, Groenink, and Dimon – he or she is acting neither for the long-term welfare of the company nor in the interests of its shareholders.

Top managers, personal assistants, and supervisory boards may mutate into agents, which can have a negative effect:
- Favoritism: Individuals who are in the boss's circle or enjoy his or her favor receive preferential treatment.
- Friend-enemy formula: People who do not like the boss are considered to be against his or her entire circle and are treated accordingly.
- Yes-sir culture: If the boss wants something to be done, it is not questioned but rather carried out.
- Ends culture: Nothing is impossible, everything is implemented – the ends justify the means.

- Wellness culture: What the boss likes is a blessing for all.
- Positive thinking: The weighing of risks and possible dangers is not positive. It distracts from the pursuit of profit or from doing what the boss wants.

Agents in the broader sense also include flatterers, who Maurice Joly described almost 150 years ago as follows:

> There is a tendency to take the view that the great positions are occupied by great talents, in the same way as events are attributed to great origins. […] However, it is overlooked that the law of sympathy and not that of abilities decides whether people give or deny support to one another. [...] People who need others have only one possibility of getting them to the point where they are serviceable to their interests, namely, by pleasing them. This is sufficient for explaining the success of mediocre individuals, wherever and whenever they are found.[140]

As early as 500 years ago, Machiavelli showed the way to guard against flatters:

> Because there is no other way of guarding oneself from flatterers except letting men understand that to tell you the truth does not offend you; but when everyone may tell you the truth, respect for you abates. Therefore a wise prince ought to hold a third course by choosing the wise men in his state, and giving to them only the liberty of speaking the truth to him, and then only of those things of which he inquires, and of none others; but he ought to question them upon everything, and listen to their opinions, and afterwards form his own conclusions. With these councillors, separately and collectively, he ought to carry himself in such a way that each of them should know that, the more freely he shall speak, the more he shall be preferred; outside of these, he should listen to no one, pursue the thing resolved on, and be steadfast in his resolutions. He who does otherwise is either overthrown by flatterers, or is so often changed by varying opinions that he falls into contempt.[141]

Rapture

This has to do with top managers becoming ungrounded when they over-estimate themselves. Rapture is used figuratively, as a metaphor, and is associated with the vertical, i.e., with hierarchy and power.

Top managers become ungrounded and enraptured, losing touch with the base, when they no longer know what's happening beneath them – where, how, and which contracts are being negotiated, deals are being done, risks are being evaluated, and products are being manufactured or sold, in other words, where the true added value for the company is being generated. The reasons for this are diverse: insufficient prioritization of their activities, insufficient knowledge, insufficient sensibility, or targeted concentration of power in the hands of the bosses and their agents. However, this does not mean that top managers need to be aware of everything going on in the company. That would overwhelm both the system and the managers themselves and ultimately be counterproductive. What needs to be emphasized here is that top managers should be in tune with their companies to such a degree that they know where, how, and by whom the outcomes are generated that are relevant to success.[142]

Which of our CEOs knew what was happening in his company day to day? Did they have an understanding of modern financial products? Did they make an effort to find out how credit default swaps are generated? Fuld, for whom an elevator was sequestered when he arrived at headquarters so that he could go up to his floor by himself and to whom access was controlled solely by Gregory, his COO, acted in an isolated, aloof manner and presumably remained fixated on the knowledge he acquired in the 1970s and 1980s.

Did Jamie Dimon know what kind of deals Iksil was making in London?

Rapture can also mean that top managers or top bodies fail to or inadequately implement controls, monitoring, and oversight. Controls are implemented not because there is a lack of trust in employees but rather due to the responsibility for the company associated with the job.

It is considered established that controls were missing for Kerviel. Either his direct superiors were professionally incompetent or the responsible internal control organs failed to heed the various warning signs. It is also possible that management granted Kerviel a free hand because it expected further profits from the "rainmaker" and therefore charitably overlooked irregularities and his failure to take vacation. Between 2005 and 2008, the controlling department at UBS employed several thousand people.[143] I have to ask myself which projects these people were looking at during this period. At UBS during this time, it seems that little heed was paid to examining and approving new financial products.[144] The reason why Ospel didn't take seriously such critics as the chief economist and the COO of U.S. operations may also be attributable to the fact that he didn't want to hear it (like Fuld) or that these critics couldn't get past his agents. The same presumably occurred in the autocratically led banks of FitzPatrick, Groenink, Goodwin, and Corzine.

To me, the statement by Jamie Dimon on his double role as chairman and CEO seems ungrounded, as he stated about the New York Federal Reserve's board: "It is not like a board. It is more of an advisory group, in my opinion."[145]

In my opinion, our case studies, as well as the hearings by the U.S. Congress on the financial crisis, reveal a lack of self-criticism. None of our top managers have publically admitted that they themselves made any mistakes. Fuld even claimed that to his dying day, he will never understand why the government didn't bail out Lehman Brothers like it previously had done with Bear Stearns and then AIG. The fault always lay with others: the government's financial policy, competitors, or the market, where no one could possibly have foreseen such a dramatic change, especially because of computer models and rating agencies, etc. When everything was going swimmingly and success was tangible, the top managers considered this to be due to their personal involvement; when not, the problem lay with other people or *the system*. In my view, this is a special form of irrational behavior.[146]

Large sections of the financial economy, in particular, global banking institutions, as well as legislatures, oversight authorities, and rating agencies, need to face the blame for the financial crisis, as was expressed by Klaus Schwab in his opening remarks to the World Economic Forum in January 2009:

> Today, people from every corner of the globe ask how it was possible that decisions could be taken, led by greed or incompetence and with no effective oversight – decisions that had terrible consequences, not only for the global economy but also for real people [...][147]

Since then, the crisis has intensified, but it has not lead to any fundamental rethinking of the behavior of top managers in the financial industry.

The main criticism relates to top management, i.e., members of management boards, supervisory boards, and the management committees of banks. They have failed to carry out their obligation to ensure the long-term future of their companies in the interests of their employees, as well as of state and society. This is because they were too committed to their self-interest and allowed the speculative use of capital to get out of control in relation to the capital used in the real economy.[148]

For this reason, it is important to address in detail in the next chapter the question of who is responsible and in what way: What type of top managers do we want? Who is responsible for their education and training? What is the role played by schools and universities? What do financial companies have to do going forward in order to better fulfill their responsibility to state and society, and which checks and balances and corporate governance structures should they outfit themselves with in order to generate crisis-resistant decisions by their top managers? And how is this change in organizational culture to be achieved?

3 Findings: Who has responsibility, and in what way?

Taking responsibility means having answers and drawing conclusions.[149] Being responsible moreover means being accountable for having decided in a particular way in a certain situation and not otherwise. One is either self-aware and in control or instead becomes absorbed by an attentive, powerful organization.

3.1 Managers – Self-aware and in control or overestimating themselves?

How can we be self-aware and in control of ourselves when we generally tend to overestimate ourselves and our abilities? This applies particularly to the estimation of our abilities as managers. In 2010 I invited 25 executive-level managers from Deutsche Bank to take part in an assessment. Also participating in the online survey were members of middle management from the health-care sector, the oil industry, the media, logistics, and IT. In all, some 120 managers from a variety of companies and sectors participated in the assessment.

The participants were given a code that they used to access a series of questions on the website of a consulting firm. After a brief introduction, questions about various areas of management had to be answered, such as motivation, delegation, coaching, influence, communication, etc. What made the survey interesting was that the first question always read: "Motivation – On a scale of 1 to 10, how do you rank your ability to motivate others?" Or: "Delegation – On a scale of 1 to 10, how do you rank your ability to delegate tasks to employees?" In other words, the issue was estimating one's own abilities and scoring them. Following the introductory question, specific questions were asked about the respective area, such as: "Costs need to be cut in your organization. How do you motivate your employees to take part in the cost-cutting program while still continuing to do their jobs well? Or: "What are the criteria you use when delegating tasks?" The responses to these questions were rated by the consulting firm, likewise on a scale of 1 to 10. The average score for the eight questions was compared to the self-evaluation. Overall, the results for all participating companies were roughly the same. The surveyed individuals gave themselves a score of between 7 and 8.5. The scores given by the consulting firm to the specific questions were considerably lower, between 3.5 and 5.5.

While the consultants' assessments were based on a series of questions, they were of course not always objective. In some cases, very precise responses were expected. They were pursuing the aim of showing us where a need for action was and how this could be addressed – by their experts – with corresponding training and coaching. A similar result was reached in a survey of more than 2,000 employees in Great Britain: Whereas 80% of the managers believed that their employees were satisfied or even very satisfied with them, only 58% of the employees agreed with this estimation.[150] This makes it clear that we are generally too optimistic in the estimation of our management abilities.[151] We view ourselves in a much too positive a light and think that we're good, well-regarded executives.

Why is that? Why are we so certain that we're good managers when we in fact make many mistakes? Why do we overestimate ourselves? In evaluating whether someone is an expert, the so-called 10,000 hour rule has become established in science,[152] according to which at least five hours per day over six years is necessary in order to become an expert in a certain field. Gladwell cites many individual examples, from hockey players to the Beatles to Steve Jobs. In every case, existing talent found a favorable environment. However, great effort and hard work, day in and day out, were required in order for those talents to become recognized, successful experts.[153] At first glance, one might get the impression that managers have an advantage. Let's take the example of a 38-year-old bank director: He's been in the business for 13 years and has led teams for the past 11 years, first with 2 employees, then with 7, and for the past 3 years with 25. In addition, he was captain of his soccer team for three years while in college. This talented man has easily accumulated the six years that are apparently needed in order for a manager to become an expert. But this appearance is deceiving, and these are the possible reasons:

- First, the ascent and success of a hockey player, the Beatles, or Steve Jobs is comprehensible, even provable. The skater plays in the NHL, the Beatles broke records in music sales, and Steve Jobs built a computer empire. Likewise, our manager pursued a career. He was promoted from analyst to director and became responsible for an increasing number of people on his team or teams. But his successes can't be measured quite as clearly. Are they attributable to his expert knowledge or to his leadership commitment? Does he owe them to favorable market conditions or to his employees? Did serendipity play a role? One might object here that this could also apply to the Beatles or Steve Jobs. However, musicians and IT entrepreneurs are normally not judged as managers but rather almost exclusively on the basis of the results they achieved in their particular market segment (number of records sold and sold-out concerts; profits earned and the company's market cap).

- Second, the question arises as to whether the 14 years during which our manager had been assigned leadership responsibility are sufficient in order to cover the required six years of practice. This is doubtful. Based on my practical observations, I consider it unlikely that he has spent five hours a day with issues of management. The requirement constantly advocated by leadership consultants that managers invest 30% of their time in day-to-day leadership runs aground amidst the plethora of daily demands, both routine and unexpected, which the individual normally deals with more as a specialist than as a manager.

- Third, I have determined that in everyday leadership, many managers generally spend too little time on management issues. They don't read any management literature (books handed out by the CEO at regular intervals to directly subordinate top managers adorn their shelves unread; internet links provided by HR to articles about management issues are rarely visited), and they spend little time reflecting about their own leadership style and actions. Management simply happens, just like the way we eat and drink: We do it, but we're not very aware of it, we don't think about it too much, and we're not very self-critical.

- Fourth, we managers don't get enough unfiltered feedback about our behavior and our actions as leaders. People smile at us when we arrive or praise the talk we gave yesterday to the staff, but no one tells us about things that didn't go so well or what others are saying about us. On the other hand, the feedback that an athlete or a musician receives comes in loud and clear. If the hockey player goes several games without scoring or loses the puck too often, he can be relegated to the minor league. If the pianist plays Chopin waltzes too quickly, too slowly, or with too many mistakes, he won't be appearing any longer on the world's concert stages. A manager, on the other hand, can't always be judged in the same way. Even worse: Normally, our belief gets reinforced that we are truly good, which then leads precisely to this false self-assessment that was shown by our experiment and the survey.

- Fifth, it might be that the 10,000 hours represent only a sort of practical part and that special, meaningful experiences are also needed in order to become an expert in management matters. I'm thinking here, for example, of key personal experiences that cause one to reflect, that help form one's identity, or that call into question one's own actions. Looking back at my own work as manager, the following experiences might fall into this category, although I by no means claim to be an expert:

  - As a lieutenant, I was proud to be promoted to captain and take command of a mechanized infantry unit. This also meant saying goodbye to my company and moving to another battalion. When I reached my new unit, I was amazed to find a completely different culture – one that was foreign to me (atmosphere, relationship of non-commissioned officers to commissioned officers) – that I first had to gain access to before I could positively change it.

  - In my book on leadership in war,[154] I did extensive research and conducted numerous interviews. The personal descriptions by war veterans preoccupied me for days and nights on end and henceforth significantly influenced my style of leadership.

  - During an exercise with a subordinate battalion, my brigade had a serious accident. I agonized over this, and I asked myself and my staff whether we were partly at fault or partly responsible and what precautions we should take in the future to prevent such incidents.

  - The replacement of a top manager in connection with restructuring in our division at Deutsche Bank caused considerable uncertainty and anxiety with some employees. Many looked to me, the non-banker, for advice and leadership. Although I was not prepared for it, I had to get used to this (new) role quickly.

Researchers are predicting that technology will someday replace all human abilities. However, they claim that six abilities will survive, regardless of how fast and intelligent computers may become. In their view, these six basic human abilities cannot be mimicked and will never be able to be performed by computers: analyzing data critically, understanding and solving complex problems, convincing people, supporting people, controlling processes involving group dynamics, and writing well.[155] Even if I factor out the last ability, it is nevertheless clear that all other abilities have to do with classic management responsibilities. I conclude from this that only a person can lead other people, that only a person understands the fundamental responsibilities of management, and that only a person can influence other people with respect to a certain goal or performance. The word "management" is derived from the Latin words *manus*, meaning "hand," and *agere*, meaning "to act." Management is an inherently human endeavor, whose purpose is to show others the way or to take them by the hand. In my view, it is thus associated with special values, such as respect, dignity, care, and self-determination. In order to lead, one has to both like and need other people, since nearly every service provided is the product of human thinking and action. In addition, management has to be understood as a process that is driven by people and dependent on a variety of interactions.

Being an expert is not enough. The management process requires patience, tenacity, humility, and self-criticism, as well as the willingness to listen and observe, and to reflect on and learn from one's actions and those of others. Such institutions as family, school, and university are intended to support this process. And organizations are supposed to create a corporate governance structure and a company culture that provides for checks and balances and facilitates learning. I will address these and other issues in the following sections.

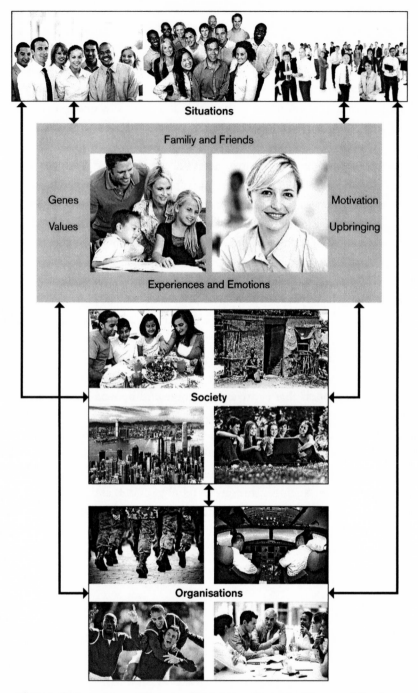

Figure 2: Interplay of People, Situations, Organizations and Society (Photos; istockphoto.com)

3.2 Top managers – What kind do we need?

Thomas Hürlimann compared today's cosmopolitans with those who lived in the ancient world and had the following to say:

> The modern cosmopolitan feels at home on level ground, everywhere on the planet's surface. But the cosmopolitan in ancient times moved not so much horizontally but, to reduce it to its essence, vertically, between heaven and earth, between the one small point and the entirety of the universe. He travelled not in the breadth but rather in the expanse, in the height.[156]

Might it be that top managers are today's cosmopolitans? They spread their reach of power horizontally. They conquer new markets, fly all over the world, communicate at all hours of the day with everyone of importance to them. Are they lacking the vertical? Quoting Hürlimann, have they taken their leave of metaphysical spheres and become self-determined individuals who serve only themselves with carte blanche?

Multidimensional set of concepts

To me, a horizontal and vertical cosmopolitan seems to be the type of top manager that we should strive for, since this individual can draw on a multidimensional, rather than a one-dimensional, set of concepts. A set of concepts means assumptions and categories that we use to interpret and assess our world and make decisions. Our sets of concepts tend to take root, and to this extent, they condition us and our destiny. This proposition can be traced back to Aristotle: We orient our actions according to concepts in which we comprehend the world. And every decision that we make based on our conceptual framework tends to reinforce our set of concepts, in that it is confirmed and stabilized by these actions. These thoughts are based on talks with Manuel Bachmann, who advocates the following proposition:

> If one has a more comprehensive, more reflective system, he possesses a greater degree of freedom, which is more appropriate to the ambiguity of the world. In unclear situations, he has a greater number of alternative interpretations at his disposal. In competitive situations, he can factor the opponent's set of concepts into his own. And the capacity of the set of concepts to be reflective assures that

his position will be qualified and enhanced. To this extent, our sets of concepts are a tremendous resource available to us, one that we are barely aware of.

This approach is directed against unreflective, monofunctional, static strategies for success that view success solely as a function of performance or the right methodology or which presume that available outside resources and circumstances or an inner nature, e.g. genes, are decisive for success. While this approach does not seek to deny these other aspects as factors for success, it does seek to strongly qualify them and to augment them through reference to the power of our sets of concepts, about which Hegel says: "The absolute power in us."

Some sets of concepts are more comprehensive than others. One example of this is the Copernican Revolution: The heliocentric view was able to become established, because thanks to the more comprehensive set of concepts, it was also able to integrate the geocentric one. There are unreflective and reflective sets of concepts. For example, science's set of concepts versus that of mythology: The latter cannot reflect upon the fact that there are alternatives to the mythological view of the world. Science, on the other hand, is able to do so because it can classify mythology as an historical antecedent, as an independent approach to the world, and as an alternative to science itself and thus can put itself in context.[157]

Why is it that the Arabs did not respond to the discovery of America with their own expansion and colonization, even though in the late 15th century, they were politically, culturally, and militarily superior to the Europeans? Instead, they colonized only parts of Africa and Asia and had a set of concepts that did not require the category "New World" because they were in control of all trading routes from Asia to Europe. This one-dimensional set of concepts made it impossible for them to properly assess the strategic and historical importance of the discovery of America. We reach a similar conclusion when we consider China. During the second half of the 19th century, the Chinese became a pawn in the confrontations between European powers. Because China considered itself the Middle Kingdom, standing at the center of the world and viewing other cultures as barbarian, it felt it needed only itself and paid no attention to developments in other countries.

Unreflective and static sets of concepts in the case studies

Those who unilaterally see success in personal profit (money, recognition, esteem) and ignore other factors on the market and in government, politics, and society are incapable of switching over to a reflective, dynamic set of concepts when circumstances change. The set of concepts conditions the way in which decisions are made and actions are taken.

Homo oeconomicus is a misleading approach, not just because its rationality has as such been exposed as a fiction but also because this rationality relates only to the individual and his or her benefit, thus creating a one-dimensional set of concepts. The rationality of the individual in combination with the "invisible hand" of the market does not stand up to the reality of the modern world and is of no use in developing tomorrow's top managers.

Critical reflective rationality

For this reason, we should strive for a type of top manager who reacts to the challenges of the global economy with a comprehensive, multidimensional set of concepts and relies on critical reflective rationality when making decisions and taking actions. One who draws on a diverse wealth of education and experience. One who is not constrained by recourse to their own individual rationality and just a few dimensions, such as money making, and career, status, and recognition in their own, isolated (financial) world. In the cosmopolitan of ancient times, I see top managers who have been trained in both heart and mind and who can draw on a number of experiences and concepts in their actions. This includes a well-rounded education, interest in new and unknown things, the ability to engage in dialogue, and life-long learning. Kitted with these abilities, a top manager is capable of making critically reflective, rational decisions.

Management as process

You are not born this type of top manager, however you can be developed into one. It is a process that begins very early in childhood and adolescence and continues for the rest of your life. Individuals and organizations influence this development and mold the individual. We can distinguish between various phases in which their influence as well as their responsibility emerges.

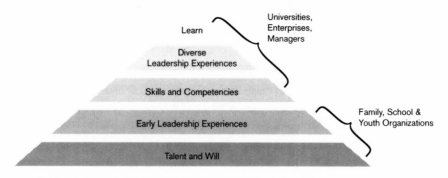

Figure 3: The formation of a manager

Talent and will

Talent, in the sense of inherent ability, is necessary. It is often the case that talented leaders are recognizable by the fact that they seek responsibility. These individuals are not satisfied with simply doing their own jobs but rather want to get involved to a greater degree and voluntarily take on responsibility. They don't shy away from personal effort and go about their work in a spirited manner. They display courage, i.e., they are not afraid of stepping on anyone's toes, and they don't avoid difficulties. They can be enthusiastic and are capable of imparting upon others their inner joy about an endeavor.

Will is a drive emanating from within to go out on a limb, to take on additional assignments, to accept success and failure as such, to derive consequences for follow-up assignments, and to be prepared to work for the organization at a different location or in a different culture.

Just as there are inherent talents for musical or athletic pursuits, there is also a talent for management. The rudiments of this can be observed in children, for instance, how they interact with others their age or take part in games. Whereas some tend to stick to a passive role, others constantly invent new games or readily assign their friends to groups and call the shots. This is where initial experiences are made in dealing with people and thus with leadership.

Experiences can be lasting when they take place in a structured environment. Schools (consider the class president, to name one), sporting groups, scouting associations, etc. are organizations that assign institutional management tasks and in this way offer young people the opportunity to gather initial experiences.

Leadership experiences

Professional leadership experiences have a special value, since this is where performance can be assessed and verified.[158] Much like in adolescence, where the parental home plays a formative role, the first 10 to 15 professional years are very important. Decisive during this period is how many opportunities are afforded to lead company units and whether these are marked by success or failure. In this regard, it is not just the successful phases that count foremost. It may also be interesting to see how junior managers respond to a setback, for example, failure to get a promotion or a relatively unsuccessful posting abroad: Do they give up, or do they draw the necessary conclusions and try again? The optimal method is allowing a young executive to gradually assume more responsibility with respect to the importance of the job and the number of subordinate employees. In this regard, global organizations have a considerable advantage.

In addition, leadership experiences gained outside of the profession are important, because they show the manager in a different organization, in a different environment, or in interaction with differently motivated people. And every further act of leadership can enrich the personal wealth of experiences as manager.

Learning and the ability to learn

The foundation of management knowledge can be learned. The manager's tools include, for example, leading oneself, holding meetings, and giving talks. Managers can learn to plan their own time according to priorities, that meetings have a structure and clear sequences, and that presentations (with or without PowerPoint) demand certain technical expertise, for example, with respect to slides, visual aids, and oral presentation. These techniques can be learned and practiced. In addition, general knowledge in the area of corporate leadership and management can be acquired.

The ability to learn relates not just to taking in, processing, and implementing management knowledge but also to the analysis of one's own leadership experiences and those of others. Biographies about personalities and case studies about companies might be useful. Reflecting about one's own actions and a healthy feedback culture in organizations can help in preventing the same mistakes from being made and in anticipating potential threats. As managers get older, especially as they climb higher up the career ladder, formalized learning in the sense of taking courses occurs less frequently. As individuals ascend higher in an organization's hierarchy, they become more unwilling to be confronted with the unvarnished truth, or to put it differently, they hear fewer negative things about themselves and their team, because employees have either too much respect or too much fear to speak openly. It may be a kind of timidity when employees opt not to burden the top manager with negative things, but it may also be unbridled fear that they'll lose their jobs if they express criticism. Top managers have to be aware of this and work actively to counter it by being critical about themselves, remaining modest, and embodying a culture in which mistakes can be discussed and reservations or differing opinions can be expressed without having to expect personal consequences. Only actions are capable of convincing employees, words alone are not enough. In particular, top managers must also learn to listen and observe, as well as to think about their own behavior and the reactions of other people.

3.3 Family, school, and youth organizations

It is impossible to over-emphasize just how strongly parents, family members, friends, acquaintances, youth organizations, and schools influence the formation of one's personality. Whether intended or unknowingly, a variety of individuals and groups, some more clearly than others, mold tomorrow's leaders. Although people are capable of constant development, the first 20 years of life are especially important. In this regard, personality is more or less strongly influenced particularly in the following areas: empathy, social interaction, and values. How does the individual approach other people? How much credit of trust does he or she give them? What role does he or she claim in a group? What values does he or she bring to these relationships? For their part, the people that influence him or her originate from an ethno-social and religious group and live in a state imbued with history and culture. These communities mold the people living in them. Everyone has an impact on everyone else and is in turn influenced by them. These interactions determine a significant part of the personality of the top manager-to-be.

Values embodied by parents and the support they give their children create the foundation for many later developments. The family is very significant, not just generally in values-based child-rearing but also specifically in the assumption of responsibility, for instance, in a youth organization. It is frequently the parents who encourage their children to join an association – and take on a leadership role, even though that is not said so expressly. All activities that are directed toward leadership commitment offer practical experiences in management that can be built upon later.

Parents as mentors

I was impressed by the story of Manuela from Australia, who was considered at Deutsche Bank to be a respected young manager with development potential. She described to me her background over a cup of coffee:

> I became a Girl Scout at an early age. At 14 I became a Senior and two years later, an Ambassador. I talked a lot about it with my father, a factory director. I first learned about the Girl Scouts from him, and he would often tell me things that were going on at work. I could talk to him about everything, and he gave me a lot of advice, like when I became editor of the school newspaper in high school. As editor, I was often at odds with the school administration and the students. But somehow I did it. When I went to college, I had to move to Melbourne. I lived in a dormitory, where I took the job of dormitory director. The job happened to be open and no one wanted it. That allowed me to earn money to pay for part of my tuition. There was a lot to do and many problems to solve. I spent a lot of time talking, convincing, and settling disputes. I even had to arrange for all the cleaning and parties. But it was a lot of fun, and people said they were happy that I was here. That gave me confidence.

Listening to her, it comes as no surprise that today Manuela has become a manager who is esteemed by both her superiors and employees. She was talented and had repeated opportunities to take on leadership tasks and prove herself in a variety of roles. And one thing stands out: She had a mentor, her father, who encouraged her and to whom she could turn.

Youth leaders and teachers

Youth organizations, like sports associations and Boy Scouts/Girl Scouts, mold the behavior and actions of children and adolescents. This has less to do with learning a specific sports technique, physical endurance, or, as with Boy Scouts and Girl Scouts, orienteering. Young people are influenced primarily by coaches and camp leaders, who give inspiration through their words, behavior, and actions. They are, in the truest sense of the word, mentors for adolescents. On the soccer field or at summer camp, they impart values – whether consciously or unconsciously is irrelevant. Values are simply imparted. Not infrequently, adolescents bear these in mind for the rest of their lives.

Molding is accomplished in a similar fashion, though perhaps in an even more intensive, lasting way, by teachers, particularly those who teach the final years of school. Which teachers do young adults remember the most? Which ones mold them in the most lasting way? It is rarely those who have an amazing knowledge of their subject but instead those who are charismatic, who fascinate young people, who turn chemical formulas into a voyage of discovery or history classes into an adventure in bygone times thus inspiring reflection upon the present. They win over students not through their expertise but because of who they are, because they find the right tone, listen to students, are open to one-on-one talks, and provide advice, assuming they are asked for it. They don't avoid conflict, don't barricade themselves behind their subjects. Teachers who positively influence and mold us act true to the motto, "Book learning may fade, but the example remains."

Against the pupil mentality – A plea for early leadership experiences

The above-mentioned complexity as the basic pattern for the daily working life of managers, as well as the demand for a multi-dimensional set of concepts, should ideally lead high schools to encourage thinking in context and to reward extracurricular activities, for example, as young entrepreneur, youth leader in sports associations, newspaper editor, bandleader, or theater director.[159] This could be accomplished through a special mention and acknowledgment in the student's school record with corresponding contribution to the overall grade. I am aware that this is not an easy task and that it can't be done with the grading system traditionally used in high schools. And of course students primarily need to perform scholastic work in order to achieve a high school diploma. However, in my view, a pure pupil mentality cannot be in the interest of politics, firms and society. One does not become a responsible citizen and manager solely through scholastic achievements but rather through early adoption of responsibility in the conflicting priorities of performance and people, as well as through corresponding support, encouragement, recognition, and the occasional admonishment. Aren't there at least two or three teachers in every high school who are able and willing to accept this challenge?

Countries in which military service is an established component of society offer many good possibilities for gathering management experience. In Switzerland, young adults can learn leadership tasks in the militia army as officers. In hands-on exercises with soldiers, 20-year-olds learn to stand in front of people, inform them about actions, and assign tasks to them. In this environment, it quickly becomes clear whether they are up to the task or not. Thanks to a healthy feedback culture, their experiences are transformed into know-how that, while not able to be adopted later in their careers simply at face value, does in fact constitute a good basis for developing further into a manager. And in this environment, young people likewise learn how to handle small setbacks and defeats and deal with frustration, which can only be beneficial for a later career as manager.

Experiences vary from individual to individual

Everyone has their own experiences and can relate both positive and negative examples. Gerald Hüther tells a particularly impressive story:[160]

While on a train, Hüther meets a lawyer, who notices the title of his talk, "Children need roots." The two travelers start talking. Hüther emphasizes the importance of relationships that offer security during childhood in terms of a person's later development. However, the lawyer is unimpressed by the reference to well-documented scientific studies and claims to be living proof that this is not accurate. Now, the professor listens intently to the lawyer's story: Following his birth, his mother couldn't cope with him and developed a psychological illness. His father abandoned the family when he was very young, and he never learned what became of him. He was sent to stay with an aunt, who struggled with him for six months. He was told that he was colicky which exasperated his aunt. She sent him on to other relatives, who likewise couldn't cope with him. So he was sent from relative to relative until at about the age of three, he landed in an orphanage as a child with behavioral problems. This was the start on an odyssey, from orphanage to orphanage, all across Germany. Prior to reaching puberty, he had spent time in a dozen of these institutions, never staying longer than one year in any of them. He said that what he (Hüther) had written in this book was in fact true for most of the children that he had met in these orphanages. They had become troubled individuals, often drop-outs, and many of them did indeed turn out to be asocial, addicted to drugs, or criminals. But that didn't happen to him. He got his high school diploma, studied law, and made something out of his life. ... But there was one positive experience in his childhood that gave him the strength to discover and follow a path that was different than that of his classmates. When he was about 10, he met a teacher in one of these orphanages who was completely different than all of the others. He was the first person he had ever met who really looked at him and accepted him for who he was. He can't remember which classes this teacher taught, only that all of a sudden, school and learning started to become really enjoyable. Somehow, this teacher was able to awaken in him the feeling that he was truly important, that he was capable of doing things, and that it was very enjoyable to be curious and discover the world. After six months, he had to leave for a new orphanage. But he never lost his passion for learning, and ever since, he has cherished the memory of this one, decisive teacher. It was as if this teacher had put him on a different track and given direction to his life. Moreover, he had tracked down the teacher several years ago in order to express his gratitude with a bouquet of flowers and a bottle of wine. He thanked the teacher, now over the age of 80, for his openness and warm-heartedness. The teacher wouldn't have any of it: He said that he had had so many pupils over the years and that he couldn't quite remember him, the lawyer.

3.4 University economics departments and business schools

University economics departments, above all, business schools, are responsible in part for manager training. Professors have to impart and demonstrate not just knowledge relevant to the working world but also how to think in contexts and to act on the basis of values. Networked research projects and interdisciplinary seminars support a broad, multi-dimensional, scientific education.

Universities, particularly business schools, have occasionally been accused of being partly to blame for the financial crisis.[161] Among other things, it is claimed that they had placed too much emphasis on specialized knowledge and on methods like best practices instead of fostering the ability of students to think and their analytical capabilities.[162] It is asserted that instead of case studies and pat formulas, they should be imparting the passion for asking questions and starting dialogues. By all means, best practices have their positive side: Stories from the real world are told that are interesting, authentic, and often inspiring. Case studies aren't taken from the remote past but rather from the current economy, and they involve top managers who are well known from media exposure. However, best practices become problematic when they end up being pat formulas or models for courses of action, with the only reason for applying them being to become successful. In the process, independent thinking gets short shrift, although this is essential in order for managers to analyze complex situations in their organizations and to make pragmatic, rational decisions.[163] In addition, this masks conflicting priorities that are primarily personally motivated, which everyone has because they are molded by genes, family, society, and organizations.[164]

Relevance to practice and role as forward thinker

Looking just at best practices is not enough when it comes to reforming university economics departments and business schools. In my view, they should once again pay more attention to practice and take on the role of forward thinkers. This does not mean that the teaching of specialized economic and financial knowledge should be ignored. Rather, the interrelationships between market, society, and state, as well as the neurological conditioning of *homo sapiens*, need to be accorded greater weight, as does the dialogue about potential socioeconomic and political trends and the challenges these present for management.

In my view, the orientation of research toward publication in so-called A journals also needs to be called into question. Articles are published in A journals only if they have been reviewed in advance by renowned professors. While that may certainly promote the quality of academic research, nevertheless only a small circle of specialists is involved in the discourse. It is questionable whether the scientific community should be both creating and judging objective truth. Although in politics we keep careful watch over separation of powers, this apparently does not exist in the academic world.[165] There is a real danger that discussions will ignore the actual problems facing management. Perhaps these are considered to be too banal or not worthy of academic discussion. Nevertheless, I believe that university instructors should once again spend more time taking the pulse of the economy and its managers. In too many instances, their contacts are limited to HR management, from which they obtain company figures and the results of employee surveys. Indeed, many HR professionals often share the same fate as their academic partners: The live in an ivory tower, detached from management on the frontlines. They alone are not to blame for this – it can also be traced back to the corporate governance of companies: the global heads of HR rarely have a permanent seat on the executive committee; their budgets are the first to be sliced when cost-cutting takes place; division heads tend to circumvent their company-wide HR plans and make direct contact with external trainers and coaches; the company's guiding principles announce that they put people first; and the corresponding deeds are unfortunately non-existent. HR management then becomes involved in its own marginalization when it confronts the business with too many demands or with designs that are too elaborate or lack practical relevance, when it does not implement enough initiatives and achieve enough results for business, or when it is too involved with itself.

Questionable ratings

Earlier, I described how rating agencies were involved in the financial crisis and bear some responsibility for it. The situation is similar with institutions that made it their job to select the supposedly best business schools. They are partly to blame for the unilateral academic direction of elite business schools. For instance, in 2012 the Financial Times was still ranking the top 100 MBAs by such criteria as salary (three years after graduation), career progress, percentage of women faculty and women students, internationality, and languages.[166] My criticism is directed less against these criteria than against the absence of the following ones: courses involving general management, ethics, interdisciplinary case studies, and dialogue with politicians.

Training students how to think and to engage in constructive discourse

In my view, it would be advantageous to create anonymized case studies that are relevant to practice. While they should be based on actual events, they shouldn't pretend to offer solutions for outside of the classroom. They should focus on analytical and critical thinking and on discussions, not on the listing of pat formulas in the sense of best practices. The aspects of irrationality on the part of top management, as outlined in chapter 2.8, are likewise suitable for training purposes. Each of the areas has positive and negative attributes. Some people may be highly structured and consider themselves less susceptible to being blinded by past successes. Others are more serious and reserved and think they are less at risk of acting in an emotionally charged manner. But who would admit to a weakness for the erotic appeal of others?

This doesn't have to do with an emotional striptease but rather with thinking: reflecting on the conflicting priorities to which top managers are exposed in certain situations and organizations, debating motivating and risky aspects of management, and using forward thinking with respect to one's own behavior in various situations and companies.

Encouraging independent thinking takes one beyond conventional ways of thinking and the boundaries of one's own area of expertise. The issue is promoting a decision-making culture in the sense of critical reflective rationality – not to be confused with acting as a know-it-all and nagger – as well as a dialogue with employees and dissenters.

Promoting understanding for state and politics

The state–company relationship can't be simply reduced to such issues as paying taxes and ensuring the viability of the location, nor is it based solely on a company's own actions concerning corporate social responsibility. Essentially, at issue here is the role of managers as representatives of companies and as citizens. They have the following obligations: to their company and to the state in which its headquarters are based, as well as to countries in which the company conducts business; to be loyal, to treat representatives of the state with respect; and to obey the relevant rules. Every company is also part of a state and must submit to its laws. The fact that companies pay millions in taxes and thus contribute to the welfare of the state should not mislead one into seeing only the financial aspects of the relationship. Top managers have to be aware of their companies' shared responsibility to the state and act accordingly: create jobs, promote the common good, and be mindful of the environment. Their demeanor and behavior toward politicians should be characterized by self-assured modesty and interest. As CEO, Marcel Ospel often showed himself to be rather insensitive toward politicians in Zurich, the location of UBS's headquarters: He appeared late for meetings with city government officials and barely concealed his lack of interest in local matters. The American Brady

Dougan is distinctly unfamiliar with the institutions and advocates of the state of Switzerland, where the headquarters of Credit Suisse are located, and this doesn't seem to bother him in the least. And when a top manager of a private bank says that "only idiots pay taxes," it is unsurprising that the public begins to lose faith in bankers. In cases such as these, professors should take a clear stance and not shy away from describing to their students the consequences of such words. They have to help students gain insight into the interrelationships and interactions between top management, society/politics, and organizations. Professors in Switzerland should feel all the more reason to do so given the fact that this country is a democracy and politics establishes the basic conditions for the economy. In Switzerland, citizens do more than simply go to the polls every four years to elect the executive and the parliament – they also regularly give their opinion on issues. The people rule, and it is they who are responsible for the political checks and balances. In my view, the democratic form of state offers the optimal setting in which the free economy can thrive and basic conditions can be established that are fair and equitable for all citizens.[167]

Holistic management training

Starting with basic university education, and later in business school programs, it is important to stress the manager's actions and behavior. The findings of, inter alia, brain research, psychology, history, sociology, and philosophy must be taught in such a way that both prospective and experienced managers alike can gain insight into their own behavior and the way they affect people and organizations.

In my view, it is never too early to start making prospective managers aware of their responsibility. Beginning in the first semesters, students should be informed about the conflicting priorities of management and the importance of a multi-dimensional, reflective set of concepts, and using interdisciplinary case studies, they should be trained to think in contexts, options, and alternatives, as well as on how to act in a manner oriented to practice. To this end, company internships are helpful and for this reason should be a part of the curriculum at university economics departments.

3.5 Companies

Organizations exercise considerable influence on their (top) managers. They determine in large part the images that managers and employees have of both the organization and themselves, the guard rails within which they can move, and the grammar underlying their communication. In short, companies create the basic conditions for decisions and actions by their managers. For this reason, there is great significance attached to the vision, strategy, and values that companies adopt, as well as to the structures, decision-making power, and supervisory and control mechanisms they establish on the normative level. In this way, images are specified that, in turn, shape the organization's culture.

Regulating power

Companies are obligated to regulate power with checks and balances and, using corporate governance,[168] to establish strategic guidelines in terms of comprehensive company management. In my view, these include the following institutional rules:

- Composition and duties of the management and supervisory board: These are to be filled with top managers selected not on the basis of discretion or personal relationships but rather pursuant to a list of requirements approved by the general meeting of the shareholders.
  - Diversity: One or two members of the management board and the supervisory board should come from other market segments, because they are able to contribute other points of view and judgments to discussions or spot potential dangers lying outside of the company's own market.
  - Professionalism: Multinational companies, or "organizations of experts,"[169] with thousands of employees have virtually a right to be led, controlled, and supervised by professional management boards and supervisory boards. Individuals who simultaneously serve on multiple management boards or supervisory boards are unable to concentrate sufficiently on this very important task.
  - Separation of powers: An individual who sets political requirements for an organization or is part of that organization is not well suited for a position on the management board or supervi-

sory board. Double appointments as board chairman and CEO must be avoided, other than for only a brief interim period, as when succession is being arranged or the company's survival is at stake.

  – Strategy: The management and supervisory board discuss and make decisions about strategically relevant matters that are their exclusive domain. This creates a counterweight to the CEO and company management, which then orient their actions according to the decisions handed down from above and concern themselves with operational matters.

- Term limits: This must be looked at closely, since, as described above, habituation and hubris can prevail over time with top managers. Eight to ten years seem to me to be an appropriate period of time for taking a position of power, serving the company, and creating added value for stakeholders. Limiting U.S. presidents to two terms of four years each is a moderate, wise rule. How often have we seen that after ten years, many formerly exemplary officeholders now consider themselves to be like the Sun King, making decisions that are primarily designed to keep themselves in power? They no longer inspire the organization or adapt to a changed environment, yet they deal with the media in a superior, magisterial manner. The long terms of office of Fuld, FitzPatrick, and Cayne confirm this comparison to the Sun King. Politics provides similar examples, such as the former German chancellor Helmut Kohl or the former Swiss energy and transportation minister Moritz Leuenberger, both of whom were in office for more than 15 years and missed the right time to make a more dignified exit.

- Innovation management: It would be wrong to reduce the management and supervisory board to their control functions. These are of course important with respect to setting rules, but that is not enough. Both boards must also contribute to increased value by, for example, providing management with an outside view, raising awareness of risks that have emerged in other sectors, or exchanging information with individuals from the public sector or politics about possible developments and trends.[170]

- Systemic diversity: Organizations should ensure healthy diversity that is intrinsic to the system.[171] Diversity has many names: women in the company's highest governing bodies and, in general, a high percentage of women and older men in management positions;[172] promotion of cultural and ethnic diversity in leadership positions;[173] and internal mechanisms, such as after-action reviews and lessons-learned – processes or audits that are designed to help the organization learn from past failures or near-failures and to make adjustments where needed without assigning blame. Diversity then becomes a part of the organization's culture when it is accompanied with and supported by trust and respect. If an individual is given a chance and is listened to, he or she will be prepared to take a stance. The behavior of top managers has a corresponding signal effect.

- Rules about decision-making power: The company stipulates the kinds of decisions that may and must be made by each executive level of the organization. In this regard, it is necessary to define which decisions are normative, strategic, or operational. This might not always be clear in practice, and decisions sometimes need to be made on an ad hoc basis in order to avoid losing any time. But the mere fact that there is a rule and corresponding executive bodies or executive levels facilitates review and possible modification. In addition, it stabilizes and harmonizes the organization's culture.

- Culture of awareness, transparency, and the willingness to learn: Today, many modern companies have to operate with a high degree of reliability. I include among these organizations of experts, e.g., nuclear power plants, aircraft carriers, hospitals, drilling platforms for extracting crude oil on the high seas, and financial institutions. Within these organizations of experts are, inter alia, one or more control centers that have monitors displaying information relevant to the smooth functioning of operations. All data, work processes, and operating statuses capable of being recorded are visible or accessible. Day and night, 365 days a year, correspondingly trained specialists keep an eye on the monitors and all deviations from normal status. They work in shifts. In the event electricity is lost, back-up generators are available. The IT used is state of the art. Thick manuals contain checklists for a wide variety of breakdown scenarios. But nevertheless, problems always crop up, and sometimes there is even a catastrophe. Why? There are essentially three reasons for this. First, the environment in which these organizations function is highly complex. It is impossible to predict all possible breakdowns and crises, nor can preventive measures be planned for every scenario. Second, even the most modern information technology gives us access only to that data which we consider important or correspondingly register. There may be loopholes: it may be that the information technology doesn't deliver any data or that instruments show a normal status when in reality there are errors occurring in the system. Third, the monitors are operated by humans. We humans occasionally make mistakes. "To err is human," goes the saying. We forget something or make a clumsy movement. We didn't do so intentionally, but it happened. When there is pressure to perform, stress can occur, just like when we have to work long hours and get too little rest. Stress and lack of sleep generally lower the quality of our work. We lose concentration, no longer see all the data, no longer control things precisely enough, and therefore make mistakes. Many accidents in organizations of experts are attributable to human error. Boredom also plays a role. Usually, an investigative commission is then put together to analyze what went wrong and find out which individuals are to blame, who are subsequently put on trial and pilloried by the media. But naming, blaming, and shaming is not the right approach for ensuring that organizations of experts operate reliably and safely. Instead, top managers can mitigate these risks by delegating decision-making responsibility to those people who are experts and are close to the "frontline" or the customer, promoting diversity, anticipating that mistakes will happen, and institutionalizing a culture of awareness, transparency, and the willingness to learn.[174]

I would like to illustrate the last point with an example: As mentioned, an aircraft carrier is an organization of experts consisting of about 5,000 men and women and more than 100 aircraft. Individual or systemic errors can cause serious accidents. For instance, a nail lying on the deck can cause a flat tire, leading to uncontrollable events when a fighter jet tries to land. It might crash into the water or skid into the control tower, thus shutting down the entire system.

A sailor crosses the landing platform. Suddenly, he sees a long screw. In essence, he has three options: a) ignore it and keep walking, b) pick it up, or c) kick it away with his boot. If he chooses to do b), he again has three options: a) throw it in the nearest waste can, b) bring it to the commanding officer, or c) keep it as a souvenir. If he again chooses to do b), the organization has properly trained and managed its employee.

By picking up the screw, the sailor showed that he was aware of the danger that it could cause. And because he brought it to his superior, he showed that he didn't have to worry about being laughed at or accused of blame. He is aware that his organization has to live up to high standards and that for this reason, near-mistakes also have to be analyzed and made public, without looking for those at fault for it. The important thing is making sure that such oversights, like leaving a screw lying around on the flight deck, don't happen in the future. For this purpose, it will be necessary to hold an after-action review, where such questions are asked as: Is this kind of screw missing somewhere? Who crossed the deck with tools and accessories? What can each crew member do in their respective areas in order to ensure that the flight deck stays clean?

The top managers' job is to support their organization in terms of the fore-going criteria. Above all, it's up to them whether the indicated measures work, since their management style either helps shape the culture or undermines it. For instance, the officers on board the ship California didn't dare wake their violent-tempered, authoritarian Capitan Lord. Their ship was close to the Titanic, which had been sending distress signals, and could have rescued many, if not all, of the 1,600 people who in April 1912 lost their lives when the supposedly unsinkable ship went down.

Training responsibility

This has many sides and consists of a number of levels. The main thing is assigning rights and duties vis-à-vis the company, for instance, with respect to the entitlement to, and obligation to take, annual vacations and the prohibition on accepting gifts or self-dealing. In addition, this involves the company's values, such as leadership principles and diversity/gender management. Another level consists of the organization's culture, how employees are expected to treat one another so that near-mistakes, mishaps, and risks can be detected early on and brought to light, without the messenger of the bad news being threatened with sanctions. This also includes imparting the basic outlines and values of the company's corporate governance.

The former CEO of Société Générale, Daniel Bouton, was wrong when he said in a newspaper interview that he cursed the day when his staff hired a certain Jérôme Kerviel. What he's overlooking is that his company had failed to provide Jérôme with additional training during his years of employment and to impart to him the bank's values and company culture.[175] Just as short-sighted were the statements by Marcel Ospel, in which he claimed that employee training was less important than recruiting the best people on the market and paying them appropriately for their performance. My experience over the past years has shown that recruiting employees from within the company and then training them is preferable to external selection. More than 80% of managers trained by us are successful in a challenging position, while only about 50% of externally recruited managing directors lived up to their name.

> In early 2009, a former staffer in Blackstone's financial advisory group was charged by the Securities & Exchange Commission with insider trading. He is alleged to have helped his parents and friends make $3.6m on information he was privy to while working in Blackstone's London office, according to the suit filed in US District Court in New York. In a letter to his investors, Steve Schwarzman, Blackstone's founder and chief executive officer, said he was "both saddened and outraged" by the news. The general counsel of one of Blackstone's principal rivals said, "We all have cultures which don't tolerate these practices." In his letter to investors, Mr. Schwarzman added that he personally made it "an absolute priority to speak to each new class of analysts and associates about the prime importance of protecting confidential information and guarding against insider trading."[176]

It is to be commended when the top manager communicates with employees at the base level. But why does the CEO speak only to them and not to his managers? It is middle management, the direct superiors, who are exposed and need support from higher levels. They need to know not only what is expected of them but also how to create a culture of trust and impart values. The CEO must pass this message on to the entire top management, too.

What kind of training makes sense?
On the one hand, we are told starting in childhood: "Practice makes perfect," and "No pain, no gain." We learned this first-hand: When we sat down and crammed our vocabulary, texts, or formulas, we passed a test.

When we practiced our tennis backhand over and over for several days, we noticed that we were making progress. The situation is similar in all areas that involve motor or cognitive skills. If you make an effort and train, you'll see positive results in the medium to long term. On the other hand, we occasionally also have sobering experiences, for instance, when we send employees to expensive, time-consuming training sessions for the purposes of preparing them for a new assignment or improving the way they deal with people. They come back to work full of drive and enthusiasm, but after a few weeks, we find that old habits start to re-emerge, and we ask ourselves what we accomplished with all the effort. We are then reminded of the "training lie,"[177] of the sort of drivel that is churned out in the name of training employees and with which thousands of consultants and coaches make their living. And we are reminded of the findings of modern brain research, which teaches us how difficult it is to change the personality of adults.

Selection of top managers

Above, I tried to explain that we tend to conform our behavior and be accommodating to our superiors. We want to please the powerful, who prefer eager, good-natured managers who implement their ideas without question. That is understandable; it's part of our nature.

However, one of the big problems this causes is the selection for top management. Is the knowledgeable, solicitous manager really the right choice? What does the company need to do in order to stop cliques from forming and to prevent mediocrity at the top? In addition, it needs to be taken into consideration that when it comes to filling top positions, personality and leadership qualities become exponentially more important than expertise and specialized experience.

For this reason, I recommend that candidates be given either a challenging, cross-divisional project or a special assignment in new surroundings to see if they measure up to their performance in day-to-day business. When faced with an unknown environment and new actors, it often becomes apparent whether the highly touted manager is up to the task and is able to achieve tangible success. Another promising option is testing candidates in an in-house training program in which unusual situations are simulated. During these one-day training sessions, participants and their teams are presented with complex, unclear situations, and their decisions and actions are observed. It is advantageous to hold these training sessions at the end of a busy work week, when participants are already tired and have to deal with additional stress. Being observed by your superiors and personnel trained in psychology tends to up your adrenalin. These simulated exercises reveal a manager's true personality and true leadership qualities. Indeed, we tend to fall back into our original patterns of behavior when we're out of our comfort zone, where we can't use or hide behind our specialized knowledge. The same thing can happen if we act according to tried-and-true patterns, instead of in keeping with the situation, when we're under stress, in a hurry, or over-tired. When people are placed outside of their own field of expertise and familiar environment, it becomes clear who is capable of making decisions that are in line with objectives, in the sense of critical reflective rationality, and of collaborating with others and achieving expedient results. Not everyone who proves their mettle in this type of simulated exercise will necessarily master real crises. But based on my many years of experience, when people show glaring weaknesses here, they are unsuited for top management. My findings reveal that roughly one third of individuals proposed by their superiors fall into this category.

My friend Urs proudly told me about a three-day trip to northern Italy that the CEO had invited him and four colleagues to join him on. "So what will all of you be doing there?" I asked. "Well, we'll take in the sights, eat at nice restaurants, and, oh yeah, pay a visit to some company. It promises to be a pretty cool trip," answered my friend. When he returned, Urs gave me a rundown. "It started out great. We visited Florence. Late in the afternoon of the second day, we got a pretty boring tour of a company with 250 employees that makes important equipment components. My God, it was so hot, and the head of the company blathered like a soccer commentator. We were compensated for our efforts with a grand, six-course dinner. Then at about 1:00 AM, over coffee and cigars, the CEO got up and said he was going to bed and that he would see us at 8:00 AM in the Olympia conference room. He told us that he expected a well-reasoned argument from each of us as to whether or not we should take over the company that we'd visited earlier." "Then what happened?" I asked, full of curiosity. "I went straight to my room and got to work: discussion of issues, schedule, evaluation … just like I learned in the army. I crawled into bed around 4:30, set the alarm for

6:30, got up and took a shower, then practiced my presentation in front of the mirror." The effort appears to have paid off. Three months later, Urs was made CEO of a subsidiary in Germany.

Neither simulated exercises with intensive observation nor other stress tests offer any guarantee that the right top managers will be selected. Based on my own experience, these evaluations have an accuracy rate of about 80%. In four out of five cases, the prognoses prove to be right with respect to future management behavior. Surprises still happen, and there is no such thing as predictions that are 100% accurate, since people may react differently in new situations. Moreover, one must always account for chance, for favorable or unfavorable circumstances.[178]

Experiences of security organizations

Military and police give their employees systematic training aimed at enabling them to prevail in difficult situations, often under life-threatening circumstances. Soldiers and police officers are drilled on using weapons, equipment, and vehicles in such a way that even when they are tired, hungry, thirsty, or in danger, they are capable of operating their systems automatically, that is, without having to think first. They are supposed to have their heads clear in order to gage the opponent's reactions and then act accordingly and coordinate the deployment of their own people, always with the objective of not only surviving but also gaining the upper hand in a dangerous situation. Although all members of a troop of soldiers or a police unit generally receive one and the same training, they don't always react the same way. What is crucial, however, is not which members distinguish themselves in training through hard work or noticeable aptitude but rather which ones later excel on the job. Because of "frictions" (Carl von Clausewitz), there are always surprises here. In the novel *All Quiet on the Western Front*, Erich Maria Remarque tells the story of Corporal Himmelstoss, who works his soldiers in boot camp nearly to death in order to prepare them for the shelling at the front but then proves to be a coward when the first enemy artillery fire comes in. But the opposite also happens, when the skinny, shy soldier, who was laughed at by many during boot camp, suddenly shows unsuspected courage under fire by helping shell-shocked comrades, carrying additional gear, or launching a decisive maneuver on his or her own initiative.

Does an individual's resistance to stress and crisis increase with the number of dangerous situations he or she experiences? On the one hand, experience can lead to a certain degree of poise, to a literal sixth sense, a special kind of intuition. People like this are endowed with the potential to plan operations or conduct training. On the other hand, the defining experiences when in danger and under stress are no guarantee that they will prevail in future operations. Not only is every situation different than those that came before, but everyone presumably has their own limit of what they can endure. This is why it is understandable that old-timers are still afraid (or are more afraid). Maybe they have survived so many dangerous situations that they fear, deep down: "Someday, my number will be up."

Importance of crisis training

An impressive story involved Rick Rescorla, former head of security for Morgan Stanley in New York:

> Rick, a former sergeant in the U.S. Army during the Vietnam War, was responsible for the physical safety of the bank's 2,800 employees working at the World Trade Center. Marked by his experiences in the Army and by the 1993 bombing of the Twin Towers, he repeatedly carried out evacuation drills with the entire staff. Just imagine: You're in the middle of important client negotiations. A lot of money is at stake. All of a sudden, the alarm goes off, and you and your clients have to proceed to line up in the stairwell and wait until you get the order to march down from the 64th floor. Understandably, Rescorla's drills weren't particularly well liked. But top management supported the crotchety sergeant and let him continue with his training drills. On September 11, 2001, his persistence paid off. All of Morgan Stanley's employees survived the terror attacks, except 13 people, including Rick and five members of his security team. He had brought everyone down to safety. When he discovered that some people were still missing, he turned and went back into the building...[179]

Studies undertaken in the aftermath of catastrophes have shown that individuals who had already experienced similar situations or taken part in crisis training were more likely to survive than those without any preparation.[180] In addition, people are more likely to survive a plane crash if they think in advance about what to do in a possible crisis scenario, for example, by listening attentively to the information provided by the cabin crew or taking time to study the instructions in the seat pocket. Also more likely to survive are those who instinctively do the right thing in life-threatening situations, such as heading straight for the lifeboats (while others indifferently order another beer at the bar) or moving luggage out of the way in order to open the emergency exit (while others are still looking for their toiletries). In addition to chance and *fortuna* (Machiavelli, Frederick the Great), these individuals apparently possess a "survival" switch in their brains that they turn on at just the right time.

Airlines have had to learn some bitter lessons in order to reach today's safety standards. In addition to all of the technical improvements in modern aircraft, it is the findings in the human and organizational areas that primarily helped to increase air-travel safety:[181]

- First, simulation: Pilots regularly spend long hours training in simulators, where they are confronted with every conceivable and even virtually inconceivable situation.
- Second, communication: Crews are trained how to deal with one another when dangerous situations arise or when the pilot makes a mistake and the copilot chooses a form of escalation that enables the captain to overcome the threatening situation without losing face.
- Third, a feedback culture that permits discussion of mistakes, near-mistakes, and omissions without naming, blaming, and shaming, i.e., without individuals being accused and vilified.

In this way, airlines create and maintain a culture of openness, which is especially beneficial for overcoming crises.

Everyone apparently has abilities and drives lying dormant within them, which enable them, with or without training, to react to crisis situations in one way or another. Without corresponding information about an individual's experiences, it is virtually impossible to predict how he or she would act. Training can awaken dormant abilities and develop capabilities. The will to learn and to develop oneself remains the most important prerequisites for success in training.

Necessity of preparing for crises

Coping with the multitude of demands in everyday business should not be confused with coping with a crisis situation. Extraordinary events require much more from executives than do normal work days, which nevertheless may be subjectively viewed by top managers as crisis-like. Management boards and supervisory boards should commit themselves to confronting the company's operational leaders from time to time with crisis scenarios.[182] This does not require months of preparation. It is enough to free all members of the executive committee of their important duties for one weekday a year. The goal is to deal with a specific scenario together. Team training, led by one member of the management board or supervisory board and one or two coaches, results in many positive experiences and findings for the leadership team. In this way, these training sessions have a positive impact on the executive body's cohesion. Each crisis may take a different course, but the fact that just one nasty case has been run through will give top management courage and confidence in handling a real crisis.

Events – Sense and nonsense

In addition to training and coaching, companies often extol events as motivational and promoting team-building. These events do not include year-end celebrations or company dinners. Rather, they involve riding down a river in a six-man rubber raft; crossing a glacier and rappelling down crevasses; tandem parachute jumping; surviving in a remote region; etc. I can't deny that I'd find some of these activities exciting, others much less so. You'll undoubtedly feel the same way. And this is precisely the basic problem with these events: Some people, probably the head manager, will feel at ease and see everything as promoting team-building. Others will feel uncomfortable or even become afraid, which turns the event into an ordeal. Moreover, these events have little to do with everyday work life. There is a risk of it being a waste of time and effort and that the group experience that was supposed to reinforce team-building is quickly forgotten when back at work, fading away as a fairly useless experience.[183]

Sensible events are those that help participants to master current and future challenges, in other words, that are directed at company-specific aims and tasks. Choosing a venue away from the company is helpful, as is a common meal. A walk in nature or a short hike through an inspiring area can help get the body moving and thus stimulate the mind, which engenders constructive discussions.

3.6 Top managers

Top managers are treated by the media and the general public as stars, as long as they are successful. They are seen within the company and by their managers and employees as teachers, because they exercise influence not only on account of their performance, but also through their behavior and actions. Top managers should be aware that they are constantly being observed. Consciously or unconsciously, managers who report to them adopt their behavioral mannerisms and expressions and mimic the way they dress, speak, compose emails and presentations, and treat employees. Although in most cases – fortunately – top managers aren't identified with completely, they nevertheless exert enormous influence on their colleagues.

Words and deeds have signal effect
The following example illustrates the effect that top managers have on their organizations:

> The images from Abu Ghraib went round the world and shocked us. Members of the U.S. Army had tortured prisoners, thus seriously violating the rules of the international law of war. The perpetrators identifiable in the photos have since been convicted by U.S. military tribunals and sentenced to various punishments, including prison. However, their superiors in the chain of command were not tried by the tribunals. The brigade general in charge of Abu Ghraib was reprimanded for dereliction of duty, demoted to colonel, and suspended. Lieutenant General Ricardo Sanchez, commander of coalition ground forces in Iraq, later relinquished his command. In the Schlesinger Report, he was accused of signing the orders governing the interrogation of prisoners: Presence of dogs, deprivation of sleep and light, and introduction of noise were intended to cause fear, anxiety, and stress among the prisoners and make them submissive. Secretary of Defense Donald Rumsfeld was forced to resign. And what about the responsibility of the commander-in-chief, President George W. Bush? Bush expressly exempted prisoners at Guantánamo from the protection of the international law of war and, specifically, authorized interrogation techniques not protected by international humanitarian law. He thus sent signals that could be viewed by soldiers further down the chain of command as providing a legitimate basis for their own actions, which were often farther-reaching and in this case unethical.

About 70% of the development of managers takes place on the job. Here, they acquire not only knowledge, techniques, and processes but they also largely adopt the words, gestures, and leadership styles of top managers or their immediate superiors, who in turn copy their bosses. Top managers have to be aware that they send out signals. Whatever they do or don't do somehow has an effect. "The employees are as good as the bosses" and "Rot begins at the top" are seasoned (leadership) sayings.

Reflection

The automatization of decisions should be stopped. As we have seen, top managers make a variety of decisions every day, unconsciously and intuitively, by virtue of their professional experience. Their experiences and their past successes, which are coupled with emotions, may also continue to be useful, provided they take a critical stance toward them. This ability to be critical includes their willingness to periodically stop making decisions automatically and create structures that enable them to ask critical questions of themselves. Specifically, I mean the following:

I recommend that top managers schedule 60 minutes per week for reflecting. They need peace and quiet for this and shouldn't be disturbed with telephone calls and incoming email or by a BlackBerry. They should reflect on things that have occurred as well as plan ahead. Questions to be asked include: What happened? Why did it happen that way? What problems are associated with it or are pending? What are the options? Who could help me manage the tasks? What time constraints need to be observed in each case? What are the resulting priorities? How do I ensure the necessary balance, in other words, when will I take a break, exercise, spend time with the family?

Top managers can't ask themselves these questions in the rush of everyday business. They need time and solitude to do it. Experience shows that it can't be done every single day, but once a week is feasible. There are no pat formulas for where and when – that depends on the individual. For one person, the best time is Saturday afternoon, when the youngsters are taking their nap. For another, it's Thursday evening after tennis and a shower. For yet another, it's Wednesday at 6:30 a.m. in the office, when no one is there and the BlackBerry stays switched off for an hour.

Positive management culture

Top managers benefit when there is a culture of openness, awareness, and transparency in their sphere of responsibility. That is the crucial prerequisite for having employees who are innovative and critical. They will look for new solutions or point out risks only if they feel sure that this won't have a downside for them. This is easier said than done, since everyone wants to be praised and not have mistakes pointed out to them, for which they might even be responsible. For this, the top manager needs to be modest and disciplined. It has to do with a rather unstable structure that is at risk of collapsing if the manager fails to take seriously the proclaimed, extolled openness and tolerance when confronted with innovative or critical views, or dismisses them as irrelevant without explanation.

Motor of cultural change in the financial sector

The top manager should attempt to win back the lost trust of stakeholders and the political and social environment. Elements of this cultural change include in-house rules on bonus payments (such as no bonuses in the event of poor business performance), three-year deferral of a portion of compensation or expenses for top management, and insisting on a critically reflective decision-making process. They also include prompting managers and employees to interact on their own initiative with colleagues in other divisions and actively seek their cooperation, so that ideas, projects, or pending transactions have the broadest possible basis and risks are detected early on. The personal example set by top managers, particularly their deeds with respect to corporate governance and the company's values, is crucial to the success of this change.

Working relationship with state and politics

State and politics have a working relationship based on partnership with top management and exercise influence: first, with respect to the security and stability of the economic location and for the people and organizations living in their sovereign territory; and second with their laws, whether in terms of company formation or the amount of taxes. The entirety of the state's set of rules and conditions and the resulting entrepreneurial latitude influence the way in which top managers can act and organizations can develop. A mutual understanding is indispensable. Top managers should personally make every effort to develop corresponding contacts.

Health as a basic prerequisite

What can the top manager do in order to stay healthy? What keeps a person healthy? Top managers have to ask themselves these questions. Every person is different, has a specific physical and psychological make-up, and should therefore listen to body and soul. To this end, one has to pause now and again and reflect on what is good for one's self and what one would like to do. Generally, every person needs six to seven hours of sleep a night, physical exercise two to three times a week, and a balanced, low-fat diet. But what's good for one person is disliked by another. As a result, this question has to be answered on a case-by-case basis, including what's fun and what one would rather not do or eat. Management boards and supervisory boards have to stop turning a blind eye to this and instead insist that their top managers plan their time in such a way that meals, leisure time, family, and six hours of sleep a night are integrated into their personal schedules.

Frustration and anger control

Serving in a responsible position includes being able to exercise control over one's behavior and emotions. It is impossible to shut out emotions, because they automatically make themselves known. They are a part of our human make-up. Nevertheless, it is possible to become conscious of them. Over time, managers who work on themselves get to know their strengths, as well as the things that can trigger negative feelings in themselves. They can learn how to handle this and to avoid displaying unfiltered anger, frustration, or fear to their surroundings. Certain individual strategies can be developed. Sue, my assistant, sometimes said to me, "Why don't you go to the gym? That would do you some good right now." Some people call their spouses or partners and calm down when they hear the familiar voice. Others take a 30-minute break, go for a walk, or head for a certain bench in the park. Still others get a glass of water and a slice of chocolate cake and whisper to themselves, "Calm down, buddy, everything's fine." Working out, taking one's mind off things, indulging oneself with something, buying a ticket to a concert or ballgame, practicing autogenic training … (nearly) everything is allowed in order to avoid displaying negative emotions to one's environment.

Ability to learn

I consider the ability to learn to be especially important, because management is based on more than just knowledge and ability and because top managers receive less and less honest information and suggestions with respect to their behavior and actions as their careers progress. Through active observation, reading, listening, and subsequent critical reflection, they should be able to create a positive climate for learning. This does not mean that they will stop making mistakes as they get older. Just the opposite: in my view, the risk of mistakes is always present. However, top managers should reduce the risk of doing damage to themselves or their organization, much like the physician is obligated to abide by the professional ethic of "First, do no harm."

3.7   Junior managers and middle-management executives

The emphasis here is first on self-management: Managers have to be able to organize their activities, plan their time, and set priorities. This involves not simply professional activities but their entire lives. Their own needs and obligations also have to be coordinated, as well as those of their family. The manager would be well advised to keep an eye on the big picture and make sure that everything fits together. Husband and wife do not live from work alone. A balanced way of life is important for health and for performance in the company.

Relationships with colleagues and clients

Relationships with peers are not to be underestimated. First, these peers are the managers' equals, over whom they have no power of control. Managers are not in a position to order them to do something specific for their team. Second, the peers pay close attention to how their colleagues conduct themselves and what they do because in many cases the peers are also competitors for possible promotions. Third, it is often the dear colleagues who add to the "reputation bubble" – they spread stories that play a role in shaping the manager's reputation. Managers can't prevent peers from attentively monitoring them and their activities or from telling stories about them. But they also shouldn't become withdrawn, calling upon their colleagues only when they need something from them. That would be counterproductive. Instead, they should cultivate these relationships, for example, through informal meetings, the occasional chat over a cup of coffee or tea, or an unprompted phone call to pass on information, say thank you, or wish the colleague a happy birthday. What is called for is not showing inordinately friendly behavior toward peers or overwhelming them but simply a loose relationship and good collegiality.

"The customer is king." Everyone knows this saying, but not everyone acts according to it. Managers should treat clients just like they treat colleagues: with decorum and respect. Contact should be sought with the most important clients – not in a way that is pushy or seeks to curry favor but rather on a regular basis that shows dependability. One special aspect should be mentioned that differs from relationships with colleagues: In dealings with clients, managers always represent their company, too, and thus its rules and values. This point is important in that, under certain circumstances, managers should conduct themselves in a way that can be quite demanding and unequivocal, namely, when certain requirements and values are at stake that are customary in the industry or specific to the company. Even kings have to abide by these.

Relationships with superiors

The managers' superiors are key figures. Not only do they establish the work environment and the amount of effort expected, but they also shape a certain organizational culture. Conduct, wording, and taking interest in employee tasks are just as pivotal as the ability to engage in dialogue. By setting a personal example, they promote a critically rational decision-making process, as well as holistic thinking aimed at the long-term success of the company. The managers' superiors are also their partners. Together, they develop and set objectives, tasks, and structures. Partners give and take, report and listen, offer and receive advice. Where the organizational climate is positive, the manager has access to the boss, who can be won over for a certain matter or convinced of something. To do so, managers need tact, and have to be able to choose their approach deftly and tailor it to the circumstances. Sometimes, in order to achieve a goal, it is best to be direct. At other times, indirect action is advantageous. In many cases, more than one attempt is needed, and the supplicant needs more time and new ideas. It can pay off when the manager has a good relationship with colleagues and can count on their express or tacit support. A unified group of colleagues can even be extremely influential. It goes without saying that this is not a call to incite mutiny but refers to the well-known fact that when direct subordinates are unified, they constitute a power basis, for better or worse. There's no need to emphasize that the superior–manager relationship is a delicate one. Permit me to offer a list of "do nots," i.e., behavior and actions that managers should avoid in dealing with their bosses:

- First, it is counterproductive to try to influence superiors in front of others, since the former can feel pressured, exposed, or even threatened. In 1815, at Waterloo, General Gérard futilely called upon Marshal Grouchy, in front of the latter's assembled staff and other high officers, to order a *marcher aux canons*. Had Grouchy taken the advice, Napoleon would undoubtedly have won the battle. One-on-one discussions, at a well-chosen time and place, are better suited to important matters.
- Second, the subject must be carefully selected when seeking to influence the boss. It is inadvisable to try to win superiors over to the opposition when a decision has already been made by the executive committee or when it involves things that the boss can't change.
- Third, forays should be avoided that could in any way threaten the superior's position. Support can't be expected if someone's authority is weakened.

Evaluating management performance

While the manager's performance can be evaluated, this requires time and effort. In order to be effective, the various evaluations need to be scheduled in advance, and the results have to be collected over a certain period of time. The following parameters have proved successful in practice:

- Evaluation by the direct superior and by other managers: The advantage here is that superiors have a good overview of, and insight into, the work of the individual being evaluated. Normally, they are in a good position to evaluate the workload and the specific circumstances under which targets are to be achieved. Depending on the nature and intensity of their relationship with the individual being evaluated, they are capable of describing successes and failures, as well as commitment and behavior. In some cases, however, evaluations by superiors have to be interpreted with caution. Bias can play a role, for instance, where sympathy or antipathy predominates, where the superior had hired the manager for personal reasons, possibly even over the objections of others, or where the two have a close personal relationship. Other dangers include superiors in need of harmony, who go out of their way to avoid personal conflicts, or bosses who are too busy or too set in their own ways and have no time or desire to deal with the performance and conduct of subordinate managers.

- Evaluation of the company culture that the manager creates: This can be accomplished with 360-degree feedback from employees or with employee surveys. If at least two thirds of employees participate, and if the questions can be answered anonymously and are phrased in such a way as to permit meaningful assessments to be drawn for individual areas of leadership and climate, they provide a good portrait of the company's culture. Attention must be paid to the fact that in every organization, there are people who use these opportunities to settle scores, as well as to any special circumstances facing the company at the time of the survey. I'm thinking here, in particular, about times of restructurings, cost reductions, or efficiency increases, which are often associated with personal frustrations and lay-offs. During these periods, which are difficult for both the company and many individual employees, high approval ratings should not be expected. Distortions may also arise, where certain company areas that scored well under the last survey now get caught in the general wake of dissatisfaction, even though a large number of managers may have worked hard to achieve a positive company culture.

- Numerical results, such as sales figures: These include the results achieved by a sales manager, the manager of a fashion boutique, or a securities trader (and of course by their teams as well). The raw data are evidence of their performance or the merits of their products. These figures should be compared with last year's results and to those of comparable competitors. Likewise, the market situation and the state of the wider economy need to be taken into consideration. Depending on the basis used for the comparison, a higher profit or a loss would have to be qualified.

- Customer surveys: Customer service is an important component of every business. That applies not just to the true services sector, such as tourism, health care, and financial services. The way in which customers are treated, how their needs and complaints are addressed, and what they receive in return are important in all areas of commerce and the markets. Surveys directed at a specific customer segment with a response rate of at least two thirds can be an important barometer for the company culture, much like employee surveys are. They are particularly helpful in areas where there is little or no data available. I'm thinking here about HR managers, teachers, and management in the security sector. Customer surveys can shed light here on how the commitment of managers is viewed and whether the target audience is satisfied with their performance.

- Feedback reports from in-house and outside training sessions, as well as from assessments: The notation "attended" or a simple certificate is not helpful. On the other hand, testing at the end of training sessions is by all means useful for evaluating the capacity or willingness to learn. Observations made by top managers and psychologists about leadership behavior in simulated exercises during interactive case studies or at assessment centers can stimulate managers to recognize their strengths and potential for development. As for the immediate superior, these often provide valuable additional information for the overall evaluation of the manager.

I need to point out two things: First, managers shouldn't be evaluated against just one criterion. Second, it must be made clear to managers in advance how their performance will be evaluated during a certain period and what consequences may be associated with this.

In my view, the individual criteria can be weighted as follows, whereby several combinations should be used:

- Evaluation by superiors: 20–30%
- Evaluation of company culture: 15–35%
- Measurable data: 25–45%
- Customer surveys: 10–20%
- Feedback from training: 10–20%

Performance and career

Does good performance ensure career and advancement possibilities? The answer is yes and no. On the one hand, performance is generally essential. Managers who can't demonstrate performance might be promoted once or twice. But they won't make it to the top, except in cases of nepotism or favoritism, which can happen. On the other hand, the reputation bubble plays a significant role. Every manager is talked about, and there is a certain opinion about him or her. It is a mix of facts, emotions, and rumors. Appearance, private life, and anecdotal information are part of the picture, as are achievements, experiences, and performance. Calls for politically correct behavior go nowhere, since it is unavoidable that people will talk about, and form opinions about, one another, regardless of how questionable it may be in a given case. It's part of our nature. Finally, there is the issue of a person's reputation, which Jeremias Gotthelf called a "name" in his novel *Uli der Knecht*:

> When a servant works ever better, is ever more loyal and skilled, then that is his property, and no one can take it away from him, and he moreover possesses a good name, people like him, entrust him with a lot, and he has the world at his feet.[184]

Gotthelf correctly points out that there is a connection between performance and a good name. Performance shouldn't be reduced to just long working hours, good evaluations, and results. What is meant is performance in the broad sense, i.e., including demeanor, behavior toward employees, colleagues, clients, and superiors, and other personal relationships. Some managers are too focused on performance in the narrow sense and neglect their relationships with other people. Instead of chasing after the numbers, facts, and results associated with performance, they would be better served by becoming aware of the effect they have as an individual and social being. It has to do with their image. To this end, they have to invest time and move outside of their own sphere of responsibility by making contacts, showing interest for other people, and offering them support.

Performance is important, but that alone is not enough to make it to the top. Image and exposure are also important, perhaps even equivalent. Moreover, careers can't be planned. Only in part is it true that "everyone is the architect of their own destiny," since careers are also determined by circumstances, perhaps even by *krainos*, a favorable, unique opportunity. Moreover, career paths don't lead straight up the ladder. They can also develop horizontally, tail off, or even go downhill before unexpectedly regaining ground. When a door closes, a gate opens elsewhere; one who is not handed the chalice today may be drinking Champagne tomorrow. Persistence, modesty, and a bit of poise and luck are what every manager needs in order to reach the top. One might even hope that one's career path doesn't lead straight up the ladder:

> So, there is nothing better for a career than having it interrupted temporarily, for when one sees the world only from above, from the imperial cloud, from the height of the ivory tower and clout, he knows only the smile of the obsequious and their dangerous readiness: He who always holds the scale in his hands forgets his true weight.[185]

Specialists in leadership positions

There are employees in every company who gladly seek more pay and a prestigious title, but not the associated responsibility. Some of them are outstanding specialists who take their jobs very seriously but prefer to work alone. They can't be blamed for that. But in organizations, individuals should be made managers only if they can do their work together with others, i.e., if they are not just results-oriented but are also committed to employees, colleagues, and clients. This doesn't mean that specialists can't be promoted. For the company's benefit, there are positions with career opportunities for them – however not on managerial levels.

> I have yet to meet anyone who wasn't thrilled by Martin. Everyone – external service providers and employees of the company – was full of praise for the smart, good-natured, charming training consultant. His job was to organize training modules for all departments in the division. He worked largely on his own, including late into the evening when necessary or on Saturdays. He had already come to the attention of his superiors, who promptly offered him the position of Head of Training when the current boss retired. Martin proudly accepted the promotion, particularly since this came with a raise and the title of director. He eagerly plunged into the new job. The first thing he did was to invite his 40 employees to a cocktail party. But after six months, the euphoria had long since dissipated. The once dear colleagues were dissatisfied. They were seldom if ever informed about things, and they rarely received assignments or feedback from the new boss. For his part, Martin worked even longer hours, often on Sunday as well. He took over everything and tried to handle tasks all by himself. When he started having trouble with his marriage, he resigned from his position in

exasperation and left the company. The blame for Martin's failure lies not with him but with his superiors. They wrongly assumed that the outstanding consultant would automatically make an excellent boss. They failed to test him for his leadership qualities.

People who prefer to work on their own, are unwilling to delegate, and avoid uncomfortable discussions with employees will hardly grow into a leadership position, nor will leadership seminars turn them into managers. It is unlikely that special leadership courses or even an expensive, months-long MBA program can make a manager out of a specialist, an employee who for years has been working independently, or a consultant who has never before had much responsibility for other people or objectives. Years of carrying out assignments reliably and successfully as a lone wolf doesn't mean that the individual is well suited to lead a team, group, or department. Instead of placing hope in an expensive outside training program, the company is better off investing time and money in the selection process and finding out whether the candidates have the sort of talent, will, and ability to learn that is required for a leadership position and are capable of developing. This evaluation covers the candidates' entire lives. With the aid of structured interviews conducted by several members of middle and top management and by experts, as well as by obtaining references, which need to provide information about behavior in a variety of real-world leadership situations, it can be tested whether and to what degree the candidate has the required expertise.

Promoting management potential at an early stage

In my view, it pays off when young, talented professionals are given management responsibility at an early stage. It is better to give them a team with just a few employees or to entrust them with a global project than to wait around. If they are overseen by the immediate superior – and possibly even by a mentor – it becomes clear after a period of time whether they have management potential. If performance is unsatisfactory, the experiment should be terminated. After presenting junior managers with an analysis in unsparing transparency, it is best to wait awhile before giving them a second chance. One might object here that this is more like a trial-and-error method than a systematic process. In my experience, however, the program is fair, transparent, and successful, provided the entire organization takes part in it, observation and support is ensured, decisions are made quickly, and feedback is given promptly. From the point of view of the participants as well, the advantages outweigh the disadvantages, since their strengths and weaknesses are pointed out to them, thus enabling them to structure a career as manager or expert with greater precision. The chance of growing into the role of manager on the job is promising and is preferable to merely theoretical training. Of course, the optimal combination is one of doing, learning, and mentoring.

Unsuitable managers

There are also managers who fail to exercise their leadership responsibility. There are more of this type than one might imagine. Many ascend the career ladder on the basis of their education, their expert abilities, and an above-average work commitment while having little or no management expertise and/or experience. These individuals certainly make their way up the ladder by showing themselves to be impressive in their field and making themselves indispensable. But their expertise lies in specialized knowledge and in the experience associated with this, not in management. They may continue to dive into work as in the past, but they're not acting as a leader but rather as an expert. They feel more at home in their traditional field of expertise, not in the jumble of human problems, which they view as nothing but a hindrance to their work. This leads to the situation where they only bring good news to employees personally. Bad news, like a lost promotion, lower bonus, etc., is either delegated to an assistant or HR, buried in a general flood of words, or sent by mass email. These often highly paid bosses prefer to occupy themselves personally with figures, facts, documents, and statistics rather than with employees, colleagues, and clients. They lead using processes, targets agreements, and email, and they avoid human problems or instead kick them either upstairs or over to HR.

How does top management deal with them? I see three options: either it succeeds in getting the manager on the right track using clear objectives and requirements, with support from the immediate superior and possibly a coach or mentor; or it transfers him or her laterally to a new job, for instance, to a purely specialist position. If these measures don't bear fruit by a specific deadline, management should let the individual go.

4 Taking stock – Who is suited to be a top manager?

The analyzed top managers from the financial world are all a product of their own, very personal career paths in various companies, which nonetheless belong to the same economic sector. Despite individual differences resulting from their personalities, they all have several things in common that are attributable to the specific features and the intrinsic, prevailing culture of the financial sector of the last 20 years, which has molded these top managers, each in his own special way. I count among these shared aspects a strong ego fixation, as well as the drive for dominance and validation. I find few traces of self-criticism, reflection, or holistic thinking. Is there a Fred Goodwin or a Richard Fuld in all of us?[186] In addition, institutional checks and balances are missing. I nevertheless acknowledge that in other times and in a specific environment these top managers were successful and were accorded esteem by their companies and the general public. What needs to be kept in mind is that the view of individuals and their deeds is one-sided. Genes, childhood, and youth and study years, as well as, very generally, environment, society, economic sector, and organization, mold and influence the personal careers of each manager to different degrees. Premature conclusions are just as wrong as perplexity. Differentiated argumentation is essential. Nevertheless, I wish to make a few clear statements.

Management is not an exact science

There are too many elements, too many variables, that interact with one another. It has to do with people who are all unique because of their genome, their heritage, and their very personal experiences, as well as with situations that are always new and distinct. Reflected in their interaction one finds the dilemma of management: We look about for rules for good management, but we find none that can be applied promisingly at every time and in every situation. We search for constants, yet we come to discover that there aren't any that are generally valid. We'd like to provide the top manager with advice, but become disillusioned as we see ourselves struggle for answers or make mistakes. But perhaps this imponderability and unforeseeability are the very things that make the study of management so fascinating. To us, management is a multifaceted, chameleon-like activity. It is not a profession, even after successful completion of an MBA program.[187]

Management as art, craft, and science

In the words of Henry Mintzberg, management can be seen as a combination of art, craft, and science.[188] This is because some of a manager's tasks are learnable like a craft, while certain management results can be analyzed scientifically and conclusions can be drawn, but their success is not guaranteed with future applications. When we think that we've identified a certain course of action that looks promising based on empirical research, it turns out that it is of little use for the next application. Still other decisions by managers surprise us, yet they prove to be successful. There are actions that are somehow unfamiliar to us and whose roots we can't comprehend, but they turn out to be expedient in a certain situation and in a certain system. There are managers that take a stab at something and, contrary to expectations, are successful in a specific case – this is what we call "art." That's one possible explanation. Another might be that it was just a fluke or benevolent fate. At the same time, however, a not insubstantial part of management remains hidden, inscrutable, or astonishing to the observer. For this reason, management also has something mysterious about it.

Management as a combination of *necessità, virtù,* and *fortuna*

Necessità: Recognizing the factors and processes at work in society, politics, and the economy and their interactions, as well as the need to act because of circumstances, whereby in the process one must always expect the reality of irrationality.

Virtù: Acting with energy and wisdom; being capable of balancing individual power (rationality) with the *bene comune* (= critical reflective rationality)

Fortuna: Being able to seize an opportunity and bring fortune to your side; fortune (or misfortune) is not fate and does not have to be passively endured.[189]

Here as well, it becomes clear that management cannot be reduced to simply following or imitating a few pat formulas for action. Management is challenging, and success comes about neither on its own nor as a consequence of one, single decision. However, managers can be successful if they analyze as carefully as possible the given economic and sociopolitical environment (*necessità*) and act energetically (*virtù*) at the time most favorable for their venture (*fortuna*). The prerequisites for this lie with managers themselves and the organizational culture they have created. They can rely on a comprehensive, multidimensional set of concepts. They make decisions with critical reflective rationality. And they have promoted a company climate of openness conducive to dialogue that is capable of offsetting the weaknesses of managers and supporting them in recognizing reality and in acting in a timely manner.

The top manager is neither a savior nor a lone actor

He or she is the leader who contributes their own assets and abilities, serves state and society, and is responsible for performance and stakeholders. Management does not involve just one person. It has its eye on neither the heroic leader, the level-five leader, nor the charismatic leader, who guides companies by his or her own virtue.[190] Management has to do with sociopolitical, societal, systemic, and technological aspects of leadership, as well as those that are relevant to personality. Moreover, it is embedded in an environment that is conditioned, i.e., one that creates certain conditions and makes it susceptible to certain decisions. This environment is a varied mesh of political, social, cultural, societal, and systemic elements that relate to one another in ever-changing ways and make connections that in turn create new prerequisites. On the one hand, each individual manager influences the organization. On the other, each one is a cell of the system, which molds and develops them. One might see this as a completely different, irreconcilable appraisal of the position of manager in the organization. But I view it as an opportunity, since the manager and the system are in a mutual, though asymmetrical upward trajectory.[191]

Central importance of rationality, culture, and corporate governance

Top managers mainly decide intuitively and act on the basis of their experiences as human beings, experts, and leaders in a specific organization. That often works well, but not always. As the case studies have shown, there is a risk that a certain situation will be incorrectly appraised and that action will be taken based on a trusted repertoire from the past and successfully applied patterns of action. In order to prevent this, three things are necessary:

- First, top managers should regularly stop and ask themselves whether their decisions satisfy the requirements of critical reflective rationality.

- Second, every top manager is dependent on other, independently thinking individuals in their environment and on direct subordinates. This is why an atmosphere of trust and a culture of openness, transparency, and fairness are of central importance, since they permit and facilitate interventions into the manager's decision-making and action process for the benefit of the company and the social environment.

- Third, it is necessary to have independent management boards and supervisory boards that guide and supervise their top managers and create favorable conditions for the long-term welfare of their organization. They have foremost responsibility for changing the culture in financial companies. Corporate governance, checks and balances, guiding principles, visions, and strategies – and the personal example set by their top managers – influence the behavior and action of all other managers in the company. Unmistakable signs of this organizational culture are diversity in the composition of its highest governing bodies, careful selection of top management, delegation of responsibility, the ability to engage in dialogue, the reactions which near-mistakes and foul-ups provoke, the criteria for evaluating managers, internal training offerings, and the selection and nurturing of in-house talents.

Signs of instability and risks

Alarms should go off with management boards and supervisory boards when, for example, information comes to light about the following modes of behavior:[192]

- When top managers become workaholics, boast that they need only four hours of sleep, and jet around the globe nearly around the clock for weeks and months at a time;
- When top managers appear not to be tending to the long-term, healthy development of the company, i.e., when they are wedded to

thinking in terms of short-term profit and thus are not acting in the sense of critical reflective rationality;

- When top managers fail to treat others with respect, avoid engaging in dialogue, can no longer listen attentively, or can only be approached by people with good relationships with their assistants;
- When there are doubts as to a top manager's integrity;
- When top managers are not personally involved in the selection of future members of top management or only bring people on board who are accommodating to them;
- When there are signs that top managers have lost touch with reality or are disconnected from the base and the company's fundamentals, or when they, e.g., react angrily to initiatives, questions, or research of the management board or supervisory board;
- When top managers infringe the principle of corporate governance or disregard the company's values;
- When there are signs that top managers are lying;[193]
- When top managers fail to analyze near-mistakes or audits with the necessary earnestness and to draw the corresponding conclusions;
- When bad news doesn't make its way quickly enough to top management or when top management reacts too slowly to it;
- When top managers are uninterested in taking stock of things on the ground or going into details in order to understand them;
- When top managers fail to actively promote collaboration among divisions and learning from one another;
- When top managers fail to get involved in succession planning and instead let managers who are becoming a "threat" go by way of "mutual agreement";
- When top managers fail to grapple with crisis scenarios;
- When top managers fail to show interest in the concerns of politics and society;
- When top managers fail to bear responsibility for the environment.

In my view, mere suspicion suffices for the management board or supervisory board to convene a meeting as quickly as possible in order to discuss corresponding action. If they fail to do so, the "guardians of corporate governance" are violating their obligations to the company and to society, from which and for which they act.

Managers who are unable to relate to a multidimensional set of concepts, do not base their decisions on critical reflective rationality, and refuse to be bound by the corporate governance of their organization are not up to handling the complex tasks that top management brings with it.

The conflicting priorities of performance and being human – on the path to natural authority

Top managers bear responsibility. In their organizations, they are responsible for performance and for people. They are exposed to a number of conflicting priorities and are confronted with diverse ambivalences. They often find themselves caught in a dilemma. Nevertheless, they are still responsible and have to decide, act, and apply the power entrusted to them for the stability and the healthy development of their organization. They can and must delegate tasks and teams to subordinate managers, but it is the top manager who maintains overall responsibility. Moreover, top managers are embedded in a certain organizational culture, as well as in relationships with the management board, supervisory board, colleagues, clients, employees, and representatives from state and society.

Depending on the size and scope of their responsibility, there may be changes to the task profile, the manner of collaboration with various stakeholder groups, and the prioritization of the agenda. Even though there are no pat formulas for being successful as top manager, several principles have nevertheless proved themselves time and again in practice, which hold that top managers are not generally wrong when, for example, they make an effort to act as a role model, to treat others with respect, to keep their word, and to stop demanding things that common sense tells them are impossible. Management is also to be understood as a learning process. Top managers should be inspired by their work in the service of the company and, using critical reflective rationality, advocate its healthy development. Despite or perhaps precisely because of all of this energy and this will, it is advantageous for them to act self-critically and modestly, to listen, and sometimes to stop and think, as well as – also to their benefit – to nurture a climate of trust and dialogue and to support the management and supervisory board in connection with corporate governance. In addition to the will to persevere, one would hope that they are at ease in their jobs and have a sense of humor.

If top managers succeed in these areas over a longer period of time, they develop natural authority, an honor that is not based on a formal position, a title, or, money but rather is bestowed by a grateful environment on the basis of years of steady performance. A manager who commands natural authority is suited for top management.

However, that is not a definitive summary of management. That would be too simple, since natural authority might also be lost again when new conditions and challenges emerge. Much like trust, which takes a long time to win, but can be lost in an instant.

Because by our very nature, we can err and do wrong, it needs continual interest, persistent study, interdisciplinary research that takes new paths, and constant joy in practical work, with discussions and subsequent reflection and forward thinking, coupled with the power to avoid languishing after successes and/or becoming despondent after setbacks. Management is a process, a constant testing in the sense of critical reflective rationality, led by the will to achieve performance together with other people for the long-term welfare of companies and their employees, as well as that of state and society.

"The superior man is distressed by the limitations of his ability; he is not distressed by the fact that men do not recognize the ability that he has."

Confucius

Appendix

Notes

Introduction

1   Cf. Gebhard Kirchgässner, *Homo Oeconomicus: The Economic Model of Behaviour and its Applications in Economics and Other Social Sciences* (New York: Springer Science & Business Media, 2008).

2   A narrow interpretation of rationality, for example, under the *homo oeconomicus* model, can lead to irrational actions. Money per se is a rational medium that measures objects on a quantitative value scale, but it can lead to an irrational striving for gain and to bad outgrowths. Critical reflective rationality does not mean doing everything feasible but instead bearing in mind the consequences for the company and society. Cf. Silvio Vietta, *Rationalität: Eine Weltgeschichte* (Munich: Wilhelm Fink Verlag, 2012).

3   Cf. Michael S. Gazzaniga, *Who's in Charge?: Free Will and the Science of the Brain* (New York: Ecco, 2011).

4   In my view, it would be wrong to dispense with rationality as an element in the decision-making process. Cf. Michael P. Lynch, *In Praise of Reason* (Cambridge: MIT Press, 2012); Tony Jackson, "Rational Choice Model Needs Help not Coup de Grâce," September 27, 2010, *Financial Times*, www.ft.com/cms/s/0/8700a68e-c984-11df-b3d6-00144feab49a.html#axzz2cDNyP9gF.

1   Case studies – How did they decide?

5   "Billion-Dollar Bubble," March 14-15, 2009, *Financial Times Weekend Magazine*, pp. 21 et seq.

6   Id.

7   Cf. Greg Farrell, "Lynched at Merrill," January 25, 2009, *Financial Times*, www.ft.com/intl/cms/s/0/7de9ad20-eb05-11dd-bb6e-0000779fd2ac.html#axzz2cDNyP9gF.

8   Cf. Joseph Tibman, *The Murder of Lehman Brothers: An Insider's Look at the Global Meltdown* (New York: Brick Tower Press, 2009).

9   Hank Paulson, *On the Brink: Inside the Race to Stop the Collapse of the Global Financial System* (New York: Headline Publishing Group, 2010), p. 123.

10   Cf. Larry McDonald, *A Colossal Failure of Common Sense: The Incredible Inside Story of the Collapse of Lehman Brothers* (London: Ebury Press, 2009).

11   Id., p. 98.

12   Cf. Paulson, *supra* note 9; Tibman, *supra* note 8.

13   William D. Cohan, *House of Cards: How Wall Street's Gamblers Broke Capitalism* (London: Penguin Books, 2009), p. 447.

14   Cf. Tim Irwin, *Derailed: Five Lessons Learned from Catastrophic Failures of Leadership* (Nashville: Thomas Nelson, 2009), chapter 6.

15   McDonald, *supra* note 10, pp. 223-24.

16   Myret Zaki, *UBS: Am Rande des Abgrunds* (Lausanne: Tobler Verlag, 2008), pp. 189 et seq.

17   Cf. Claude Baumann and Werner E. Rutsch, *Swiss Banking – wie weiter?: Aufstieg und Wandel der Schweizer Finanzbranche* (Zurich: Verlag Neue Zürcher Zeitung, 2008), chapters 5 and 6; Lukas Hässig, *Der UBS-Crash: Wie eine Grossbank Milliarden verspielte* (Hamburg: Hoffmann und Campe Verlag, 2009).

18   Dirk Schütz, *Herr der UBS: Der unaufhaltsame Aufstieg des Marcel Ospel* (Zurich: Orell Füssli, 2008), pp. 98 et seq.

19   www.subprimelosses.com/ubs-overview.php, May 22, 2012.

20   Cf. Zaki, *supra* note 16.

21   Some competitors decided differently. In the fall of 2006, traders at Goldman Sachs warned senior management about the increasing risks associated with subprime business. Taking heed of this warning, management reacted by divesting the most toxic products by the end of 2006. Credit Suisse pursued a similar strategy and got itself completely out of the subprime business by mid-July 2007.

22   Bill Bamber and Andrew Spencer, *Bear Trap: The Fall of Bear Stearns and the Panic of 2008* (New York: Brick Tower Press, 2008), p. 131.

23   Margaret Heffernan, *Willful Blindness: Why We Ignore the Obvious at Our Peril* (New York: Walker and Company, 2011), p. 138.

24   Id., p. 92.

25   Kate Kelly, *Street Fighters: The Last 72 Hours of Bear Stearns, the Toughest Firm on Wall Street* (New York: Portfolio, 2009), p. 133.

26   David Murphy and Martina Devlin, *Banksters: How a Powerful Elite Squandered Ireland's Wealth* (Dublin: Hachette Books Ireland, 2009), p. 91.

27 Id., pp. 73 et seq.

28 Jeroen Smit, *The Perfect Prey: The Fall of ABN Amro or What Went Wrong in the Banking Industry* (London: Quercus, 2009), chapters 3 et seq.

29 Id., p. 406.

30 Patricia Crisafulli, *The House of Dimon: How JPMorgan's Jamie Dimon Rose to the Top of the Financial World* (Hoboken: John Wiley & Sons, 2009), pp. 105 et seq.

31 Cf. Paul Sullivan, *Clutch: Why Some People Excel Under Pressure and Others Don't* (New York: Portfolio, 2010), chapter 7.

32 Peter Rásonyi, "Fragen über Fragen zu JP Morgan: Der Verlust im Londoner Office der Grossbank stärkt die geplante Bankenreform", May 14, 2012, *Neue Zürcher Zeitung*, www.nzz.ch/aktuell/wirtschaft/uebersicht/fragen-ueber-fragen-zu-jp-morgan-1.16881067.

33 Christiane H. Henkel, "Ein Schwarzer Tag für JP Morgan," May 12, 2012, *Neue Zürcher Zeitung*, www.nzz.ch/aktuell/wirtschaft/uebersicht/ein-schwarzer-tag-fuer-jp-morgan-1.16860754.

34 In September 2011, Adoboli, a 31-year-old trader at the Delta One trading desk, generated a loss of USD 2.3 billion in securities trading. It is probable that Adoboli racked up losses in the relatively low-risk Delta One area over a longer period of time and kept them hidden in the hopes of making up for them. C.f. There are parallels to Kerviel.

35 Well-informed journalists started to become aware of the trades being made by Bruno Iksil, the trader responsible for the loss, shortly after he executed them in mid-April 2012. For instance, Felix Salmon of Reuters wondered "what on earth Bruno Iskil, the so-called London Whale, might be doing with his reported $100 billion bet" ("Bruno Iksil and the CHIPS Trade", April 17, 2012, *Reuters*, blogs.reuters.com/felix-salmon/2012/04/17/bruno-iksil-and-the-chips-trade/). The volume of the complicated transaction, which was probably an attempt to hedge risk in other of JP Morgan Chase's positions, was in fact much higher than the generated loss of USD 2 billion. According to Salmon, this was feasible because although the trade was "big and risky ... JP Morgan is more than big enough to hold a 5-year trade to maturity." However, neither he nor his colleague, John Carney, could offer any meaningful explanation.

36 At the time this book was completed (late May 2012), it was still unclear what further consequences were in store for Jamie Dimon and JP Morgan Chase.

37   Tom Braithwaite, "Back to the Wall," May 18, 2012, *Financial Times*, www.ft.com/cms/s/0/209c876e-a0c4-11e1-851f-00144feabdc0.html.

38   Rhiannon Edward, "Fred Goodwin: The 'Boy from Paisley' Who Found Himself at the Centre of a Global Storm," October 13, 2008, *The Scotsman*, www.scotsman.com/news/fred-goodwin-the-boy-from-paisley-who-found-himself-at-centre-of-a-global-storm-1-1136950.

39   Heather Connon, "Right Said Fred, Let's Go Dutch," April 29, 2007, *The Observer*, www.theguardian.com/business/2007/apr/29/observer-business.royalbankofscotlandgroup.

40   Cf. Peter Thal Larsen, "Goodwin's Undoing," February 24, 2009, *Financial Times*, www.ft.com/intl/cms/s/0/dbcc20aa-02a0-11de-b58b-000077b07658.html#axzz2cDNyP9gF.

41   Matthew Hancock and Nadim Zahawi, *Masters of Nothing: How the Crash Will Happen Again Unless We Understand Human Nature* (London: Biteback Publishing, 2011), pp. 166-67.

42   FSA, *Board Report: The Failure of the Royal Bank of Scotland* (London: 2011).

43   Shahien Nasiripour, "Ex-MF Global Head Claims He Warned Corzine," February 2, 2012, *Financial Times*, www.ft.com/cms/s/0/42ab5ac4-4dbd-11e1-a66e-00144feabdc0.html.

44   Cf. Marc Pitzke, "Pleite von MF Global: Der Boss, der von nichts wusste," December 16, 2011, *Der Spiegel*, www.spiegel.de/wirtschaft/unternehmen/pleite-von-mf-global-der-boss-der-von-nichts-wusste-a-804071.html; Silla Brush and Clea Benson, "Corzine Tells Senate Hearing He Didn't Order Misuse of Funds at MF Global," December 13, 2011, *Bloomberg*, www.bloomberg.com/news/2011-12-13/top-mf-global-execs-say-they-don-t-know-how-funds-went-missing.html; Norbert Kuls, "Wall-Street-Eliteschmiede: Goldman und seine Talente," November 4, 2011, *Frankfurter Allgemeine Zeitung*, www.faz.net/aktuell/wirtschaft/wall-street-eliteschmiede-goldman-und-seine-talente-11517504.html.

45   FT Weekend Magazin, 5./6. September 2009: The house that Bernie built. 30.

46   Robert Kolker, "The Impersonator," April 3, 2009, *New York Magazine*, nymag.com/news/features/55863/.

47   Cf. *supra* note 45.

48   Id.

49   Irene Frat, "Many Questions, Few Answers," February 13, 2008, *Futures Magazine*, www.futuresmag.com/2008/02/13/many-questions-few-answers.

50   Rüdiger Jungbluth, "Société Générale: Jérôme allmächtig," January 31, 2008, *Die Zeit*, www.zeit.de/2008/06/Societe-Generale.

51   Carol Matlack, "Jérôme Kerviel in His Own Words," January 30, 2008, *Businessweek*, www.businessweek.com/stories/2008-01-30/jerome-kerviel-in-his-own-wordsbusinessweek-business-news-stock-market-and-financial-advice.

52   Cf. PricewaterhouseCoopers, *Société Générale: Summary of PwC Diagnostic Review and Analysis of the Action Plan*, May 23, 2008, www.bancherul.ro/files/0805241313 report Societe Generale PwC.pdf; James Stewart, "The Omen: How an Obscure Breton Trader Gamed Oversight Weaknesses in the Banking System," October 20, 2008, *The New Yorker*, www.newyorker.com/reporting/2008/10/20/081020fa fact stewart.

53   "All His Fault: A Harsh Sentence for Jérôme Kerviel," October 7, 2010, *The Economist*, www.economist.com/node/17204665.

54   Christoph von Pauly, "Tod eines Bankers," July 13, 2009, *Der Spiegel*, www.spiegel.de/spiegel/print/d-66055466.html.

55   Kiran Randhawa, "City Trader in Death Leap Feared Sack Over Internet 'Prank'," February 16, 2010, *London Evening Standard*, www.standard.co.uk/news/city-trader-in-death-leap-feared-sack-over-internet-prank-6706573.html?origin=internalSearch.

2   Analysis – Why did they decide the way they did?

56   Kevin Kelly, *CEO: The Low-Down on the Top Job* (Harlow: Pearson Education Limited, 2008), pp. xvii-xviii.

57   Daniel Binswanger and Miklos Gimes, "Wir brauchen schärfere Regeln," May 7, 2011, *Tages-Anzeiger: Das Magazin* [subscription only].

58   Cf. Henry Mintzberg, *Managing* (Harlow: Pearson Education Limited, 2009); Emilio Matthaei, "The Nature of Executive Work," Doctoral thesis, Leipzig Graduate School of Management (Wiesebaden: Gabler Verlag, 2010).

59   Cf. chapters 2.6 and 2.8.

60   Richard Sennett, *Together: The Rituals, Pleasures and Politics of Cooperation* (London: Allen Lane, 2012), p. 175.

61 Heffernan, *supra* note 23, pp. 90 et seq.; Jürgen Zulley, "Unsere Politi-
kerinnen und Politiker schlafen zu wenig," December 18, 2011, *Neue
Zürcher Zeitung*, www.nzz.ch/aktuell/startseite/unsere-politikerinnen-
und-politiker-schlafen-zu-wenig-1.13693320.

62 Tina Groll, "Führungsstil: Entscheider suchen den Sinn," April 30,
2012, *Die Zeit*, www.zeit.de/karriere/beruf/2012-04/studie-fuehrungs-
kraefte-verstaendnis.

63 Cf. Gerhard Roth, *Persönlichkeit, Entscheidung und Verhalten: Warum es
so schwierig ist, sich und andere zu ändern* (Stuttgart: Klett-Cotta, 2007).

64 Id.

65 Id.

66 Cf. Joseph Ledoux, *The Emotional Brain: The Mysterious Underpinnings
of Emotional Life* (New York: Simon & Schuster, 1996).

67 Cf. Gerald Hüther, *Die Macht der inneren Bilder: Wie Visionen das Gehirn, den Menschen und die Welt verändern* (Göttingen: Vandenhoeck
und Ruprecht, 2008), chapter 2.1.

68 Gary Klein, *Streetlights and Shadows: Searching for Keys to Adaptive Decision Making* (Cambridge: MIT Press, 2009), p. 34.

69 Cf. Antonio Damasio, *Self Comes to Mind: Constructing the Conscious
Brain* (New York: Pantheon Books, 2010).

70 Cf. Richard E. Neustadt and Ernest R. May, *Thinking in Time: The Uses
of History for Decision Makers* (New York: The Free Press, 1986).

71 Roth, *supra* note 63, pp. 110 et seq.

72 Daniel Kahnemann, *Thinking, Fast and Slow* (New York: Farrar, Straus
and Giroux, 2011), p. 411.

73 Roth, *supra* note 63, pp. 115 et seq.

74 Bruno Frey, "Die psychologischen Grundlagen des Marktmodells,"
in *Wirtschafts-, Organisations- und Arbeitspsychologie: Marktpsychologie.
Sonderdruck aus der Enzyklopädie der Psychologie*, edited by Dieter Frey,
series III, vol. 5 (Göttingen: Hogrefe Verlag, 2007).

75 Reinhard Selten, quoted in Roth, *supra* note 63, pp. 117-18.

76 Gerd Gigerenzer, *Gut Feelings: The Intelligence of the Unconscious* (New
York: Viking Penguin, 2007), particularly chapter 9.

77 Michael S. Gazzaniga, *Human: The Science Behind What Makes Your
Brain Unique* (New York: Harper Perennial, 2008), pp. 121 et seq.

78 Stuart Sutherland, *Irrationality* (London: Pinter & Martin, 2011), pp.
11, 32 et seq., and 87 et seq.

79   George A. Akerlof and Robert J. Shiller, *Animal Spirits: How Human Psychology Drives the Economy, and Why It Matters for Global Capitalism* (Princeton: Princeton University Press, 2009).

80   Joseph E. Stiglitz, *Freefall: America, Free Markets, and the Sinking of the World Economy* (New York: W.W. Norton & Company, 2010), particularly chapters 9 and 10.

81   Kahnemann, *supra* note 72.

82   Barbara Ehrenreich, *Bright-Sided: How the Relentless Promotion of Positive Thinking Has Undermined America* (New York: Metropolitan Books, 2009); Michael R. LeGault, *Think: Why Crucial Decisions Can't Be Made in the Blink of an Eye* (New York: Threshold Editions, 2006), chapter 5.

83   Cf. Phil Rosenzweig, *The Halo Effect: … and the Eight Other Business Delusions That Deceive Managers* (New York: The Free Press, 2009).

84   Cf. Joseph T. Hallinan, *Why We Make Mistakes: How We Look Without Seeing, Forget Things in Seconds, and Are All Pretty Sure We Are Way Above Average* (New York: Broadway Books, 2009); Dan Ariely, *Predictably Irrational: The Hidden Forces That Shape Our Decisions* (London: HarperCollins, 2009); Christopher Chabris and Daniel Simons, *The Invisible Gorilla: How Our Intuitions Deceive Us* (New York: Crown Publishers, 2010).

85   For a more complete overview, cf. Sutherland, *supra* note 78; Kahnemann, *supra* note 72; Rolf Dobelli, *Die Kunst des klaren Denkens* (Munich: Carl Hanser Verlag, 2011).

86   Stefan Zweig, *Magellan: Der Mann und seine Tat*, 24th ed. (Frankfurt: Fischer Verlag, 2011), p. 87.

87   Fritz B. Simon, *Einführung in die Systemische Organisationstheorie* (Heidelberg: Carl-Auer-Systeme Verlag, 2007), pp. 24 et seq., 30; Tor Hernes, *Understanding Organization as a Process: Theory for a Tangled World* (Abingdon: Routledge, 2008).

88   Official translation of "Leistung durch Leidenschaft."

89   Passion is intended to apply more to employees and their behavior than to performance: "A passion to perform – through people and ethos," i.e., performance thanks to passionately led employees and critical reflective rationality.

90   For the definition of a psychopathic manager, cf. Adrian Furnham, *The Elephant in the Boardroom: The Causes of Leadership Derailment*

(Houndmills: Palgrave Macmillan, 2010), chapter 4.

91 Markus Städeli, "Destruktive Dynamik im Handelsraum," September 27, 2011, *Neue Zürcher Zeitung*, www.nzz.ch/aktuell/wirtschaft/ueber-sicht/destruktive-dynamik-im-handelsraum-1.12641170.

92 Cf. Sennett, *supra* note 60.

93 Cf. *supra* note 82.

94 As of late May 2012, the danger posed by uncritical management once again emerged. Jamie Dimon, who is both CEO and board chairman, said about the New York Federal Reserve's board that it is not a control and oversight organ but rather as merely an advisory body. Cf. John Gapper, "JP Morgan Exposes the Imperial CEO Myth," May 16, 2012, *Financial Times*, www.ft.com/cms/s/0/e8ea4a22-9dd0-11e1-9a9e-00144feabdc0.html. It appears that at JP Morgan Chase as well, a rubber-stamp culture has been created that puts the fate of a large company in the hands of a few select individuals, making it virtually impossible to scrutinize risky business practices. The question also arises as to whether JP Morgan Chase is simply too large and complex to be understood and run. Cf. Gillian Tett, "The Banks That Are Too Complex to Exist," June 7, 2012, *Financial Times*, www.ft.com/cms/s/0/65281562-b0c1-11e1-a2a6-00144feabdc0.html.

95 Cf. Tomas Sedlacek, *Die Ökonomie von Gut und Böse* (Munich: Hanser Verlag, 2012), chapters 8 et seq.

96 On this point, it is worth mentioning the theory of financial stability developed by Hyman Minsky, which holds that financial markets that have experienced a long phase of stability inherently become unstable and in this way cyclically destabilize stable, reliable economic systems. Cf. Cohan, *supra* note 13, p. 448.

97 Id., p. 334.

98 Nicholas Dunbar, *The Devil's Derivatives: The Untold Story of the Slick Traders and Hapless Regulators Who Almost Blew Up Wall Street . . . and Are Ready to Do It Again* (Boston: Harvard Business Review Press, 2011), pp. 246 et seq.

99 Cf. Hancock and Zahawi, *supra* note 41, pp. 15 et seq.

100 Id., p. 44.

101 Stewart Lansley, *The Cost of Inequality: Three Decades of the Super-Rich and the Economy* (London: Gibson Square, 2011), p. 21; John Plender, "Capitalism in Crisis: The Code That Forms a Bar to Harmony,"

January 8, 2012, *Financial Times*, www.ft.com/cms/s/0/fb95b4fe-3863-11e1-9d07-00144feabdc0.html; Gideon Rachman, "Why I'm Feeling Strangely Austrian," January 9, 2012, *Financial Times*, www.ft.com/cms/s/0/95d3d2c6-3ab7-11e1-a756-00144feabdc0.html.

102   Cf. Larry Elliott and Dan Atkinson, *The Gods That Failed: How the Financial Elite Have Gambled Away Our Futures* (London: Vintage, 2009).

103   Dagmar Deckstein, *Klasse! Die wundersame Welt der Manager* (Hamburg: Murmann Verlag, 2009), p. 9.

104   Plender, *supra* note 101.

105   Max Weber, *Wirtschaft und Gesellschaft: Grundriss der verstehenden Soziologie*, 5th ed. (revised) (Tübingen: Mohr Siebeck Verlag, 2002), p. 28.

106   Cf. Gottfried Koch, *Macht, Management und Verhaltensbiologie: Grundzüge eines verhaltensorientierten Managements*, Institute of Computer Science, Faculty of Mathematics and Computer Science, University of Leipzig. Manuscript [no date].

107   Cf. Heike Bruch and Bernd Vogel, *Organisationale Energie: Wie Sie das Potenzial Ihres Unternehmens ausschöpfen*, 2d ed. (Wiesbaden: Gabler Verlag, 2009).

108   Koch, *supra* note 106, p. 14.

109   Cf. Luke Johnson, "Leaders Who Use Charm to Reach the Top," September 22, 2009, *Financial Times*, www.ft.com/cms/1af05808-a7c1-11de-b0ee-00144feabdc0.html.

110   Cf. Heinrich Popitz, *Phänomene der Macht*, 2d ed. (Tübingen: J.C.B. Mohr (Paul Siebeck) Verlag, 1992).

111   Cf. Charles Handy, *Understanding Organizations: How Understanding the Ways Organizations Actually Work Can Be Used to Manage Them Better* (New York: Oxford University Press, 1993), chapter 5; Jeffrey Pfeffer, *Power: Why Some People Have It – And Others Don't* (New York: HarperCollins, 2010).

112   Jörg Albrecht, "Was im Kopf des Chefs vorgeht: Die dunkle Seite der Macht," May 31, 2011, *Frankfurter Allgemeine Zeitung*, www.faz.net/aktuell/wissen/mensch-gene/was-im-kopf-des-chefs-vorgeht-die-dunkle-seite-der-macht-1637612.html.

113   Jeffrey Pfeffer, *What Were They Thinking?: Unconventional Wisdom About Management* (Boston: Harvard Business School Press, 2007), p. 118;

Anna Catherin Loll, "Psychologie: Was Macht aus uns macht," December 2, 2010, *Frankfurter Allgemeine Zeitung*, www.faz.net/aktuell/berufchance/arbeitswelt/psychologie-was-macht-aus-uns-macht-1590134. html; Supplement C1, August 23, 2010, *WirtschaftsWoche*, pp. 79–84.

114 Cf. chapter 2.8 and the remarks on aspects of irrationality (agents).

115 Carl Schmitt, *Gespräch über die Macht und den Zugang zum Machthaber: Gespräche über den neuen Raum* (Berlin: Akademie Verlag, 1994), p. 18.

116 Cf. "Fehler bei Herz-OP," June 13, 2005, *news.ch*, www.news.ch/Fehler+bei+Herz+OP/214105/detail.htm. Two of the team's physicians received suspended sentence from the Zurich District Court.

117 Cf. Klein, *supra* note 68; Gary Klein, *Sources of Power: How People Make Decisions* (Cambridge: MIT Press, 1999).

118 Liä Dsi [Lie Yukou], *Die Philosophie Chinas: Das wahre Buch vom quellenden Urgrund* (Zurich: Diderichs, 1976), pp. 161 et seq.

119 Niccolo Machiavelli, "Discourses," in *The historical, political, and diplomatic writings of Niccolo Machiavelli*, translated by C.E. Detmold (Boston: Houghton, Mifflin and Co., 1976), Book 3, Chapter IX.

120 Winston S. Churchill, *Marlborough, His Life and Times – Book Two*, reprint (Chicago: University of Chicago Press, 2002), Book One, p. 105.

121 Sedlacek, *supra* note 95, p. 380.

122 Nando Parrado, *Miracle in the Andes: 72 Days on the Mountain and My Long Trek Home* (New York: Crown Publishers, 2006).

123 Cf. Stefan Klein, *Alles Zufall: Die Kraft, die unser Leben bestimmt*, 3d ed. (Reinbeck: Rowohlt Verlag, 2005).

124 Fyodor Dostoyevsky, *The Gambler* (Internet-based: Sovereign, 2012), pp. 28-29.

125 Cf. Kahnemann, *supra* note 72, pp. 213 et seq., as well as an analysis by the Financial Times that comes to a similar result: "Weekly Review of the Fund Management Review," February 20, 2012, *Financial Times*.

126 Hancock and Zahawi, *supra* note 41, pp. 128 et seq.

127 Cf. Philip D. Broughton, "Nothing Beats the Exercise of Judgment," September 6, 2010, *Financial Times*, www.ft.com/cms/s/0/500addf0-b9e6-11df-8804-00144feabdc0.html.

128 Salvatore Cantale, "Financial Tools Must Be Handled With Care," February 19, 2012, *Financial Times*, www.ft.com/cms/s/2/9dd4c6ee-

5414-11e1-8d12-00144feabdc0.html; Emanuel Derman, *My Life as a Quant: Reflections on Physics and Finance* (Hoboken: John Wiley & Sons, 2004), p. 261.

129 Quoting Ilma Rakusa, from her commentary in a German-language edition of *The Idiot*: Fyodor Dostoyevsky, *Der Spieler*, 2d ed. (Munich: Piper, 2008), p. 961.

130 Cf. Heffernan, *supra* note 23, pp. 183 et seq.

131 Kahnemann, *supra* note 72, p. 55; Heffernan, *supra* note 23, pp. 190-91.

132 Cf. Catherine Hakim, *Erotic Capital: The Power of Attraction in the Boardroom and the Bedroom* (New York: Basic Books, 2011).

133 Joris Lammers, et al., "Power Increases Infidelity Among Men and Women," April 13, 2011, *Psychological Science*, leeds-faculty.colorado.edu/mcgrawp/PDF/Lammers.Stoker.Jordan.Pollmann.Stapel.2011.pdf.

134 Roy F. Baumeister and John Tierney, *Willpower: Rediscovering Our Greatest Strength* (London: Allen Lane, 2012), pp. 89-90.

135 Sydney Finkelstein, Jo Whitehead, and Andrew Campbell, *Think Again: Why Good Leaders Make Bad Decisions and How to Keep It From Happening to You* (Boston: Harvard Business Press, 2008), pp. 129-34.

136 "Ergo lädt zur Orgie ein," May 19, 2011, *n-tv*, www.n-tv.de/wirtschaft/Ergo-laedt-zur-Orgie-ein-article3371466.html.

137 Cf. Pfeffer, *supra* note 111.

138 Cf. Frans de Waal, *The Age of Empathy: Nature's Lessons for a Kinder Society* (New York: Harmony Books, 2009).

139 Simon Baron-Cohen, *Zero Degrees of Empathy: A New Theory of Human Cruelty* (London: Allen Lane, 2011).

140 Maurice Joly, *Handbuch des Aufsteigers* (Munich: Piper, 2004), pp. 52-53.

141 Niccolo Machiavelli, *The Prince* (New York: Fordham University Medieval Sourcebook, www.fordham.edu/halsall/basis/machiavelli-prince.asp), chapter XXIII.

142 Sennett, *supra* note 60, chapter 5, pp. 148 et seq.

143 Hässig, *supra* note 17, p. 97.

144 Suzanne Mejer, *Chasing Goldman Sachs: How the Masters of the Universe Melted Wall Street Down . . . And Why They'll Take Us to the Brink Again* (New York: Crown Business, 2010), p. 219.

145 Gapper, *supra* note 94.

146 See David Ellerman, "Systemisch Verantwortungslos," in *Die Gazette*, vol. 33 (spring 2012), www.gazette.de/Archiv2/Gazette33/Ellerman. pdf, which looks at the problem of the detachment of action from responsibility and the consequences of this.

147 Remarks reproduced in Don Tapscott, "'The Schwab Manifesto'," *Businessweek*, January 29, 2001, www.businessweek.com/careers/man- agementiq/archives/2009/01/the_schwab_mani.html.

148 Id.

3   Findings: Who has responsibility, and in what way?

149 Otfried Höffe, "Was ist ein 'verantwortlicher' Wirtschaftsführer?" April 3, 2010, *Neue Zürcher Zeitung*, www.nzz.ch/aktuell/wirtschaft/ue- bersicht/was-ist-ein-verantwortlicher-wirtschaftsfuehrer-1.5367326.

150 Brian Groom, "Bad Managers Seen as Threat to Growth," May 3, 2012, *Financial Times*, www.ft.com/cms/s/0/bc8961b6-9452-11e1- bb0d-00144feab49a.html.

151 It also appears that CEOs generally have difficulty admitting mistakes. Cf. Lucy Kellaway, "Business Leaders Are Worse Than They Think," March 13, 2011, *Financial Times*, www.ft.com/cms/s/0/afcf160c- 4c2b-11e0-82df-00144feab49a.html.

152 Kahnemann, *supra* note 72, p. 239.

153 Cf. Malcolm Gladwell, *Outliers: The Story of Success* (New York: Little, Brown and Company, 2008).

154 Ulrich Zwygart, *Menschenführung im Spiegel von Kriegserfahrungen*, 3d ed. (Frauenfeld: Huber Verlag, 1988).

155 Cf. Executive Appointments Supplement, May 3, 2012, *Financial Times*.

156 Thomas Hürlimann, *Das Holztheater: Geschichten und Gedanken am Rand* (Zurich: Ammann, 1997), p. 12.

157 Manuel Bachmann, *Kampf der Weltversionen: Zur Logik des Pluralismus* (unpublished manuscript).

158 See chapter 3.7.

159 Gerhard Roth, *Bildung braucht Persönlichkeit: Wie Lernen gelingt* (Stutt- gart: Klett-Cotta, 2011), p. 302.

160 Hüther, *supra* note 67.

161 "Mastering Management: Managing in a Downturn," *Financial Times*

special report (2009), www.ft.com/intl/reports/managingdownturn; cf. also Della Bradshaw, "Perhaps Schools Are Partly to Blame?" January 26, 2009, *Financial Times*, www.ft.com/cms/b2bf0588-eb49-11dd-bb6e-0000779fd2ac.html.

162   Cf. Philip D. Broughton, *What They Teach You at Harvard Business School* (London: Viking, 2009).

163   Cf. Cooley, Thomas: A pioneer of analytics over anecdote. In: FT, 26. . Januar 2009. 5.

164   Bob Iger, CEO of Disney, says that in business school case studies, emotional aspects are left out of account during decision-making. Cf. Adi Ignatius, "The HBR Interview: Technology, Tradition, and the Mouse – An Interview with Disney CEO Robert A. Iger," July 2001, Harvard Business Review, hbr.org/2011/07/the-hbr-interview-technology-tradition-and-the-mouse/ar/1.

165   Sedlacek, *supra* note 95, p. 298.

166   "Global MBA Rankings 2012," January 30, 2012, *Financial Times*, rankings.ft.com/businessschoolrankings/global-mba-rankings-2012.

167   Cf. Daron Acemoglu and James Robinson, *Why Nations Fail: The Origins of Power, Prosperity, and Poverty* (London: Profile Books, 2012).

168   Cf. Helmut Maucher, *Management Brevier: Ein Leitfaden für unternehmerischen Erfolg* (Frankfurt: Campus Verlag, 2007), chapter 6.

169   Weick and Sutcliffe define organizations of experts as "high reliability organizations." These are organizations that require a high degree of security and invest in corresponding process operations and training, such as hospitals, nuclear power plants, aircraft carriers, and banks. Cf. Karl Weick and Kathleen Sutcliffe, *Managing the Unexpected: Assuring High Performance in an Age of Complexity* (San Francisco: Jossey-Bass, 2001).

170   Didier Cossin, "Corporate Boardrooms Are in Need of Education," January 9, 2012, *Financial Times*, www.ft.com/cms/s/2/796e749a-35ff-11e1-ae04-00144feabdc0.html.

171   Sidney Dekker, *Drift into Failure: From Hunting Broken Components to Understanding Complex Systems* (Burlington: Ashgate, 2011), pp. 173-74.

172   More women and older men in leadership positions means less testosterone and probably also fewer risky business practices. Cf. Gillian Tett, "Regulators Must Get Grip on Traders' Hormones," March

15, 2012, *Financial Times*, www.ft.com/cms/s/0/dee2e528-6ea7-11e1-b1b2-00144feab49a.html.

173   Leaders in global companies need "cultural intelligence." Cf. David Livermore, *Leading with Cultural Intelligence: The New Secret to Success* (New York: AMACOM, 2010). Cf. also Gene Crozier, "One-Size Leadership Model Does Not Fit All," June 13, 2011, *Financial Times*, www.ft.com/cms/s/2/6d86ce1e-9372-11e0-a038-00144feab49a.html.

174   Cf. Weick and Sutcliffe, *supra* note 169; David D. Woods, et al., *Behind Human Error*, 2d ed. (Burlington: Ashgate, 2010); James Reason, *Managing the Risks of Organizational Accidents* (Burlington: Ashgate, 1997); James Reason, *The Human Contribution: Unsafe Acts, Accidents and Heroic Recoveries* (Burlington: Ashgate, 2008); Olaf Hinz, "Führen in extremen Situationen," May 23, 2011, *Süddeutsche Zeitung*, www.hinz-wirkt.de/downloads/Fuehren_in_extremen_Situationen_Sueddeutsche.pdf.

175   Cf. Hugues Le Bret, *Die Woche, in der Jérôme Kerviel beinahe das Weltfinanzsystem gesprengt hätte* (Munich: Verlag Antje Kunstmann, 2011).

176   Henny Sender, "Blackstone Staffer Charged with Insider Trading," January 15, 2009, *Financial Times*, www.ft.com/cms/1c807f04-e296-11dd-b1dd-0000779fd2ac.html.

177   Cf. Richard Gris, *Die Weiterbildungslüge: Warum Seminare und Trainings Kapital vernichten und Karrieren knicken* (Frankfurt: Campus Verlag, 2008).

178   Kahnemann, *supra* note 72, pp. 229 et seq.

179   Amanda Ripley, *The Unthinkable: Who Survives When Disaster Strikes – and Why* (New York: Three Rivers Press, 2008), pp. 289 et seq.

180   Id.

181   Cf. Jonah Lehrer, *The Decisive Moment: How the Brain Makes Up Its Mind* (Edinburgh: Canongate, 2009), chapter 9.

182   Kerjan-Michel, Erwann: «Ein AR/VR sollte unkonventionelle Krisenszenarien üben, um vorbereitet zu sein.» in: FT, 19. Mai 2012. 14 (Übersetzung durch den Verfasser).

183   Elisabeth Rizzi, "Abenteuerteams haben ausgedient," April 21, 2009, *Handelszeitung*, www.handelszeitung.ch/management/abenteuerteams-haben-ausgedient.

184   Jeremias Gotthelf, *Uli der Knecht* (Zurich: Diogenes, 1978), p. 31.

185 Stefan Zweig, *Joseph Fouché: Bildnis eines politischen Menschen*, 48th ed. (Frankfurt: Fischer Verlag, 2010), chapter 4, p. 107.

4 Taking stock – Who is suited to be a top manager?

186 Lucy Kellaway, "There Is a Fred Goodwin or Dick Fuld in All of Us," March 16, 2009, *Financial Times*, www.ft.com/cms/72d4154c-11ca-11de-87b1-0000779fd2ac.html.

187 Richard Barker, "Management Can Never Be a Profession," September 5, 2010, *Financial Times*, www.ft.com/cms/s/2/e0db7430-b76a-11df-839a-00144feabdc0.html.

188 Cf. Mintzberg, *supra* note 58.

189 Machiavelli, *supra* note 141.

190 Cf. Dirk Baecker, *Postheroisches Management: Ein Vademecum* (Berlin: Merve Verlag, 1994); Barbara Czarniawska, *A Theory of Organizing* (Cheltenham: Edward Elgar Publishing, 2008), pp. 65-77; Stefan Stern, "A Question All Leaders Should Ask Themselves," December 1, 2009, *Financial Times*, www.ft.com/cms/s/0/111bc7c8-de07-11de-b8e2-00144feabdc0.html.

191 Cf. Niklas Luhmann, *Organisation und Entscheidung*, 2d ed. (Wiesbaden: VS Verlag für Sozialwissenschaften, 2006).

192 Cf. Sissela Bok, *Lying: Moral Choice in Public and Private Life*, 2d ed. (New York: Vintage Books, 1999).

193 Id.

Glossary

After-action review   Feedback method aimed at the systematic exchange of experiences. It is used, in particular, by military forces, usually directly following a mission, in the form of a team meeting. The objective of the review is to ascertain the mission's factors of success and weaknesses for all members of the task force, to identify potentials, to build on strengths, and to eliminate weak points. The individual leading the review prompts the exchange of thoughts by asking specific questions.

Amygdala   The amygdala is an almond-shaped group of nuclei located within the medial temporal lobe of the brain. It is primarily responsible for evaluating and recognizing situations, as well as for analyzing possible dangers and the resulting emotional mechanisms. For instance, the amygdala controls fear and aggression.

Autopoietic systems   Self-referential systems that on the basis of the network of their internal processes constitute compound units and demarcate the boundaries to their environments. The term comes from the Greek *autos* ("self") and *poiesis* ("creation, production"). The existence of an autopoietic system is inseparable from what it does, and this constitutes its specific type of organization.

Back office   Section of financial institutions that handles controls, documentation, and processing with respect to financial transactions concluded by traders. This includes risk management, internal auditing, HR, IT, infrastructure, and the financial area.

Bailout   Also called rescue package. Process whereby third parties, usually governments, assume and pay off debts, or the liability for them, in the event that the economy or a company experiences a crisis.

Black swan An event that comes as a great surprise to the observer and exercises considerable influence on his actions or latitude for action.

Bloomberg Information service provided by the Bloomberg company that enables, inter alia, the real-time viewing of exchange data, charts, and news. One of the most important information platforms for traders at investment banks.

Bond Term describing an interest-bearing security.

Casual Friday Custom practiced in many companies in which strict dress rules are relaxed on Fridays. For men, this usually means foregoing tie and jacket at the workplace.

Change management All tasks, measures, and activities designed to effect a comprehensive, cross-departmental, and substantively wide-ranging change in an organization in order to implement new strategies, structures, systems, processes, or modes of behavior.

Chartered accountant Term describing an auditor. An auditor's tasks include examining a company's proper bookkeeping and its annual accounts for conformity with relevant rules.

Checks and balances Supervision and control within a company. In German-speaking countries, the management and supervisory board in particular are responsible for monitoring the management committee and the board and thus ensure balanced development of the company.

Chief executive officer (CEO) Chairman of the management committee, managing director of the board, or manager with sole signing authority.

Chief financial officer (CFO) Commercial manager or director of finances on a corporate board.

Chief operating officer (COO) Lead manager in charge of operations at large, global companies. Main duties include management, control, and organization of all processes and operational activities (but not strategic planning). Normally, CEO and COO work together closely.

Chief risk officer (CRO) Lead risk manager in a company whose main task is to estimate the risk of potential threats and damages for the company.

Collateralized debt obligation (CDO) Overarching term describing a financial instrument that is part of the group of asset-backed securities and structured credit products. CDOs consist of a portfolio of fixed-interest securities.

Commercial paper trader Trader of special securities, normally bonds, that are issued in order to obtain short-term financing.

Corporate governance Legal and factual set of rules governing the management and supervision of companies.

Corporate social responsibility (CSR) Entrepreneurial responsibility to society, which describes the voluntary contribution that a company makes to sustainable development going beyond statutory requirements (e.g. taxes).

Credit default swap (CDS) Credit derivative that enables default risks associated with loans or bonds to be traded or secured, as the case may be.

Critical-reflective rationality   Critical self-application of reason-driven thinking, which also covers a delimitation of one's own activities and the weighing of their future consequences.

Derivative   Collective term for securities whose price is dependent upon or derived from one or more underlying assets. It includes warrants and options containing special rights that are usually traded on exchanges.

Diversity management Promoting staff diversity in terms of, e.g., gender, age, sexual orientation, or origin.

Electronic trading   Electronic trading of equities, debt instruments, currencies, metals, commodities, and their derivatives.

Emotional marker   Memory associated with emotions

Executive committee   Management body or control committee in companies that normally advises or even supervises the management committee or the board with regard to important decisions.

Financial Services Authority (FSA)   British authority responsible for regulating and supervising the financial services industry in the United Kingdom.

First do no harm   Ancient motto by which a physician is to help and not harm the individual entrusted to him.

Front office   Section of financial institutions that maintains contact with clients and handles capital market transactions (arranging for equity and debt financing for clients)

Gender management   Part of diversity management, but with sole focus on gender. In many financial institutions, the interest here is in increasing the share of women in leading positions.

Government bond Fixed-income security issued by the state.

Groupthink Process by which a group of essentially experienced, expert individuals makes poor or unrealistic decisions because each individual tailors his own opinion to the presumed opinion of the group.

Group treasurer Individual responsible for the area or department that ensures that a company or a bank has sufficient liquidity at all times, invests excess liquidity in conformity with maturities, and sees to compliance with capital requirements.

Hedge fund Investment fund that is usually financed only through wealthy investors (investment per investor normally over CHF 1 million), works with little of its own money, and is characterized by very high leverage. These funds often rely on speculative investment strategies. Hedge funds offer the opportunity to achieve very high yields and carry correspondingly high risk. What sets them apart is that following the financial crisis, more than half of globally active hedge funds had to be liquidated, without small savers suffering losses.

Homo oeconomicus Actor who acts rationally and in his own interest, maximizes his own benefit, reacts to shifting restrictions, has fixed preferences, and is in possession of (complete) information.

Homo sapiens Man.

Initial public offering (IPO) Term describing a company's first issue of shares on an exchange.

Investment banking	Section of a company that mainly handles the procurement of capital (equity and debt) for clients, bank loans and structured transactions for clients as well as own trading. This also includes advisory business in connection with mergers and acquisitions.
Lessons learned	A specialized term from project management and knowledge management. After conclusion of a project, this is evaluated, and learning results are memorialized for future activities.
Leveraged buyout	Term describing the acquisition of a company using a large share of debt in order to pay the purchase price.
Maginot Line	Defensive system consisting of bunkers and other fortifications that was built along the French border with Belgium, Luxembourg, Germany, and Italy between 1930 and 1940. Named after the French defense minister André Maginot.
Mesolimbic system	Also called the positive reward system. It plays a key role in the creation of the emotion "joy." Countless drugs, like opiates, alcohol, and nicotine, also influence the mesolimbic system by directly or indirectly releasing dopamine there.
Multidimensional set of concepts	A set of assumptions and categories that we use to interpret and assess our world and make decisions.
Neuron	A specialized nerve cell in the brain for impulse transmission.
Organization of experts	Organization that consists mainly of highly specialized employees and knowledge workers, works in a risky environment, and has to provide flawless ser-

vices. They include hospitals, aircraft carriers, nuclear power plants, drilling platforms, and financial institutions.

Parietal lobe   A section of the cerebrum that plays an important role in integrating sensory information. The upper area enables spatial awareness, whereas the lower section is responsible for (spatial) processes, such as counting and reading.

Prefrontal cortex   A section of the cerebral cortex. This area receives processed sensory signals, links them with memories, and in this way initiates actions.

Private equity loan business   Term describing a form of investment capital for which the investment entered into by the equity lender is not tradable on regulated markets (exchanges).

Repurchase agreements   Term describing a short-term financing instrument with a term of generally less than one year, often only just several days or a night, and with the obligation to repurchase the sold assets at a preset price.

Shareholder value   Term describing a company's market value. It corresponds to the share price on a certain date, multiplied by the number of the company's shares that are outstanding.

Signing bonus   Term describing the fee paid to top managers when they are hired. Investment banks commonly offer this to new hires in the form of money or shares.

Stakeholder   Individuals, associations, or organizations that influence or are influenced by a company's business activities.

Subprime market	Term describing sections of the private (i.e., non-commercial) mortgage market on which borrowers with usually low creditworthiness take out home mortgages from (U.S.) banks or are persuaded by them to do so.
Synapses	Contact points between nerve cells (neurons) and other cells (like sensory, muscle, or glandular cells) or between nerve cells themselves.
Too big to fail	Companies, but also other institutions like countries or cities, that are so large that their bankruptcy is more costly for the national economy than the cost to the public to save them from bankruptcy.
Trader	An employee at an investment bank who buys and sells securities.
Workaholic	An individual addicted to work.
360-degree review	Evaluation procedure, especially for leaders, from the view of various evaluators. Characteristic of the 360-degree review is that feedback from all groups of individuals, i.e., superiors, employees, and colleagues, from the work environment of the individual being evaluated is taken into consideration. On some occasions, clients or suppliers are included in the evaluation procedure.

Bibliography

Acemoglu, Daron and James Robinson. *Why Nations Fail: The Origins of Power, Prosperity, and Poverty*. London: Profile Books, 2012.

Akerlof, George A. and Robert J. Shiller. *Animal Spirits: How Human Psychology Drives the Economy, and Why It Matters for Global Capitalism*. Princeton: Princeton University Press, 2009.

Ariely, Dan. *Predictably Irrational: The Hidden Forces That Shape Our Decisions*. London: HarperCollins, 2009.

Bachmann, Manuel. *Kampf der Weltversionen: Zur Logik des Pluralismus* (unpublished manuscript).

Baecker, Dirk. *Postheroisches Management: Ein Vademecum*. Berlin: Merve Verlag, 1994.

Bamber, Bill and Andrew Spencer. *Bear Trap: The Fall of Bear Stearns and the Panic of 2008*. New York: Brick Tower Press, 2008.

Baron-Cohen, Simon. *Zero Degrees of Empathy: A New Theory of Human Cruelty*. London: Allen Lane, 2011.

Baumann, Claude and Werner E. Rutsch. *Swiss Banking – wie weiter?: Aufstieg und Wandel der Schweizer Finanzbranche*. Zurich: Verlag Neue Zürcher Zeitung, 2008.

Baumeister, Roy F. and John Tierney. *Willpower: Rediscovering Our Greatest Strength*. London: Allen Lane, 2012.

Bok, Sissela. *Lying: Moral Choice in Public and Private Life*. 2d ed. New York: Vintage Books, 1999.

Broughton, Philip D. *What They Teach You at Harvard Business School*. London: Penguin Books, 2009.

Bruch, Heike and Bernd Vogel. *Organisationale Energie: Wie Sie das Potenzial Ihres Unternehmens ausschöpfen*. 2d ed. Wiesbaden: Gabler Verlag, 2009.

Chabris, Christopher and Daniel Simons. *The Invisible Gorilla: How Our Intuitions Deceive Us*. New York: Crown Publishers, 2010.

Churchill, Winston S. *Marlborough, His Life and Times – Book Two*. Reprint. Chicago: University of Chicago Press, 2002.

Cohan, William D. *House of Cards: How Wall Street's Gamblers Broke Capitalism*. London: Penguin Books, 2009.

Crisafulli, Patricia. *The House of Dimon: How JP Morgan's Jamie Dimon Rose to the Top of the Financial World*. Hoboken: John Wiley & Sons, 2009.

Czarniawska, Barbara. *A Theory of Organizing*. Cheltenham: Edward Elgar Publishing, 2008.

Damasio, Antonio. *Self Comes to Mind: Constructing the Conscious Brain*. New York: Pantheon Books, 2010.

Deckstein, Dagmar. *Klasse! Die wundersame Welt der Manager*. Hamburg: Murmann Verlag, 2009.

Dekker, Sidney. *Drift into Failure: From Hunting Broken Components to Understanding Complex Systems*. Burlington: Ashgate, 2011.

Derman, Emanuel. *My Life as a Quant: Reflections on Physics and Finance*. Hoboken: John Wiley & Sons, 2004.

De Waal, Frans. *The Age of Empathy: Nature's Lessons for a Kinder Society*. New York: Harmony Books, 2009.

Dobelli, Rolf. *Die Kunst des klaren Denkens*. Munich: Carl Hanser Verlag, 2011.

Dostoyevsky, Fyodor. *The Gambler*. Internet-based: Sovereign, 2012.

Dostoyevsky, Fyodor. *The Idiot*. Mineola: Dover Giant Thrift Editions, 2003.

Dsi, Liä. *Die Philosophie Chinas: Das wahre Buch vom quellenden Urgrund*. Zurich: Diderichs, 1976.

Dunbar, Nicholas. *The Devil's Derivatives: The Untold Story of the Slick Traders and Hapless Regulators Who Almost Blew Up Wall Street . . . and Are Ready to Do It Again*. Boston: Harvard Business Review Press, 2011.

Ehrenreich, Barbara. *Bright-Sided: How the Relentless Promotion of Positive Thinking Has Undermined America*. New York: Metropolitan Books, 2009.

Elliott, Larry and Dan Atkinson. *The Gods That Failed: How the Financial Elite Have Gambled Away Our Futures*. London: Vintage, 2009.

Finkelstein, Sydney, Jo Whitehead, and Andrew Campbell. *Think Again: Why Good Leaders Make Bad Decisions and How to Keep It From Happening to You*. Boston: Harvard Business Press, 2008.

FSA. *Board Report: The Failure of the Royal Bank of Scotland*. London: 2011.

Furnham, Adrian. *The Elephant in the Boardroom: The Causes of Leadership Derailment*. Houndmills: Palgrave Macmillan, 2010.

Gazzaniga, Michael S. *Human: The Science Behind What Makes Your Brain Unique*. New York: Harper Perennial, 2008.

Gazzaniga, Michael S. *Who's in Charge?: Free Will and the Science of the Brain.* New York: Harper Collins, 2011.

Gigerenzer, Gerd. *Gut Feelings: The Intelligence of the Unconscious.* New York: Viking Penguin, 2007.

Gladwell, Malcolm. *Outliers: The Story of Success.* New York: Little, Brown and Company, 2008.

Gotthelf, Jeremias. *Uli der Knecht.* Zurich: Diogenes, 1978.

Gris, Richard. *Die Weiterbildungslüge: Warum Seminare und Trainings Kapital vernichten und Karrieren knicken.* Frankfurt: Campus Verlag, 2008.

Hakim, Catherine. *Erotic Capital: The Power of Attraction in the Boardroom and the Bedroom.* New York: Basic Books, 2011.

Hallinan, Joseph T. *Why We Make Mistakes: How We Look Without Seeing, Forget Things in Seconds, and Are All Pretty Sure We Are Way Above Average.* New York: Broadway Books, 2009.

Hancock, Matthew and Nadim Zahawi. *Masters of Nothing: How the Crash Will Happen Again Unless We Understand Human Nature.* London: Biteback Publishing, 2011.

Handy, Charles. *Understanding Organizations: How Understanding the Ways Organizations Actually Work Can Be Used to Manage Them Better.* New York: Oxford University Press, 1993.

Hernes, Tor. *Understanding Organization as a Process: Theory for a Tangled World.* London: Routledge, 2008.

Hässig, Lukas. *Der UBS-Crash: Wie eine Grossbank Milliarden verspielte.* Hamburg: Hoffmann und Campe Verlag, 2009.

Heffernan, Margaret. *Willful Blindness: Why We Ignore the Obvious at Our Peril.* New York: Walker and Company, 2011.

Hürlimann, Thomas. *Das Holztheater: Geschichten und Gedanken am Rand.* Zurich: Ammann, 1997.

Hüther, Gerald. *Die Macht der inneren Bilder: Wie Visionen das Gehirn, den Menschen und die Welt verändern.* Göttingen: Vandenhoeck und Ruprecht, 2008.

Irwin, Tim. *Derailed: Five Lessons Learned from Catastrophic Failures of Leadership.* Nashville: Thomas Nelson, 2009.

Joly, Maurice. *Handbuch des Aufsteigers.* Munich: Piper, 2004.

Kahnemann, Daniel. *Thinking, Fast and Slow.* New York: Farrar, Straus and Giroux, 2011.

Kelly, Kate. *Street Fighters: The Last 72 Hours of Bear Stearns, the Toughest Firm on Wall Street*. New York: Portfolio, 2009.

Kelly, Kevin. *CEO: The Low-Down on the Top Job*. Harlow: FT Prentice Hall, 2008.

Kirchgässner, Gebhard. *Homo Oeconomicus: The Economic Model of Behaviour and its Applications in Economics and Other Social Sciences*. New York: Springer Science & Business Media, 2008.

Klein, Gary. *Sources of Power: How People Make Decisions*. Cambridge: MIT Press, 1999.

Klein, Gary. *Streetlights and Shadows: Searching for Keys to Adaptive Decision Making*. Cambridge: MIT Press, 2009.

Klein, Stefan. *Alles Zufall: Die Kraft, die unser Leben bestimmt*. 3d ed. Reinbeck: Rowohlt Verlag, 2005.

Koch, Gottfried. *Macht, Management und Verhaltensbiologie: Grundzüge eines verhaltensorientierten Managements*. Institute of Computer Science, Faculty of Mathematics and Computer Science, University of Leipzig. Manuscript [no date] (in possession of the author).

Lansley, Stewart: *The Cost of Inequality: Three Decades of the Super-Rich and the Economy*. London: Gibson Square, 2011.

Ledoux, Joseph. *The Emotional Brain: The Mysterious Underpinnings of Emotional Life*. New York: Simon & Schuster, 1996.

Le Bret, Hugues. *Die Woche, in der Jérôme Kerviel beinahe das Weltfinanzsystem gesprengt hätte*. Munich: Verlag Antje Kunstmann, 2011.

LeGault, Michael R. *Think: Why Crucial Decisions Can't Be Made in the Blink of an Eye*. New York: Threshold Editions, 2006.

Lehrer, Jonah. *The Decisive Moment: How the Brain Makes Up Its Mind*. Edinburgh: Canongate, 2009.

Livermore, David. *Leading with Cultural Intelligence: The New Secret to Success*. New York: AMACOM, 2010.

Luhmann, Niklas. *Organisation und Entscheidung*. 2d ed. Wiesbaden: VS Verlag für Sozialwissenschaften, 2006.

Lynch, Michael P. *In Praise of Reason*. Cambridge: MIT Press, 2012.

Machiavelli, Niccolo. *The Prince*. New York: Fordham University Medieval Sourcebook, http://www.fordham.edu/halsall/basis/machiavelli-prince.asp.

Machiavelli, Niccolo. "Discourses." In *The historical, political, and diplomatic writings of Niccolo Machiavelli*. Translated by C.E. Detmold. Boston: Houghton, Mifflin and Co., 1976.

Matthaei, Emilio. "The Nature of Executive Work." Doctoral thesis, Leipzig Graduate School of Management. Wiesebaden: Gabler Verlag, 2010.

Maucher, Helmut. *Management Brevier: Ein Leitfaden für unternehmerischen Erfolg.* Frankfurt: Campus Verlag, 2007.

McDonald, Larry. *A Colossal Failure of Common Sense: The Incredible Inside Story of the Collapse of Lehman Brothers.* London: Ebury Press, 2009.

Mejer, Suzanne. *Chasing Goldman Sachs: How the Masters of the Universe Melted Wall Street Down . . . And Why They'll Take Us to the Brink Again.* New York: Crown Business, 2010.

Mintzberg, Henry. *Managing.* Harlow: FT Prentice Hall, 2009.

Münkler, Herfried. *Machiavelli: Die Begründung des politischen Denkens der Neuzeit aus der Krise der Republik Florenz.* Frankfurt: Fischer Taschenbuch Verlag, 2004.

Murphy, David and Martina Devlin. *Banksters: How a Powerful Elite Squandered Ireland's Wealth.* Dublin: Hachette Books Ireland, 2009.

Neustadt, Richard E. and Ernest R. May. *Thinking in Time: The Uses of History for Decision Makers.* New York: The Free Press, 1986.

Parrado, Nando. *Miracle in the Andes: 72 Days on the Mountain and My Long Trek Home.* New York: Crown Publishers, 2006.

Paulson, Hank. *On the Brink: Inside the Race to Stop the Collapse of the Global Financial System.* New York: Headline Publishing Group, 2010.

Pfeffer, Jeffrey. *What Were They Thinking?: Unconventional Wisdom About Management.* Boston: Harvard Business School Press, 2007.

Pfeffer, Jeffrey. *Power: Why Some People Have It – And Others Don't.* New York: HarperCollins, 2010.

Popitz, Heinrich. *Phänomene der Macht.* 2d ed. Tübingen: J.C.B. Mohr (Paul Siebeck) Verlag, 1992.

Reason, James. *Managing the Risks of Organizational Accidents.* Burlington: Ashgate, 1997.

Reason, James. *The Human Contribution: Unsafe Acts, Accidents and Heroic Recoveries.* Burlington: Ashgate, 2008.

Ripley, Amanda. *The Unthinkable: Who Survives When Disaster Strikes – and Why.* New York: Three Rivers Press, 2008.

Rosenzweig, Phil. *The Halo Effect: ... and the Eight Other Business Delusions That Deceive Managers.* New York: The Free Press, 2009.

Roth, Gerhard. *Persönlichkeit, Entscheidung und Verhalten: Warum es so schwierig ist, sich und andere zu ändern*. Stuttgart: Klett-Cotta, 2007.

Roth, Gerhard. *Bildung braucht Persönlichkeit: Wie Lernen gelingt*. Stuttgart: Klett-Cotta, 2011.

Schmitt, Carl. *Gespräch über die Macht und den Zugang zum Machthaber: Gespräche über den neuen Raum*. Berlin: Akademie Verlag, 1994.

Schütz, Dirk. *Herr der UBS: Der unaufhaltsame Aufstieg des Marcel Ospel*. Zurich: Orell Füssli, 2008.

Sedlacek, Tomas. *Die Ökonomie von Gut und Böse*. Munich: Hanser Verlag, 2012.

Sennett, Richard. *Together: The Rituals, Pleasures and Politics of Cooperation*. London: Allen Lane, 2012.

Sherwood, Ben. *The Survivors Club: The Secrets and Science That Could Save Your Life*. New York: Grand Central Publishing, 2009.

Simon, Fritz B. *Einführung in die Systemische Organisationstheorie*. Heidelberg: Carl-Auer-Systeme Verlag, 2007.

Smit, Jeroen. *The Perfect Prey: The Fall of ABN Amro or What Went Wrong in the Banking Industry*. London: Quercus, 2009.

Stiglitz, Joseph E. *Freefall: America, Free Markets, and the Sinking of the World Economy*. New York: W.W. Norton & Company, 2010.

Sullivan, Paul. *Clutch: Why Some People Excel Under Pressure and Others Don't*. New York: Portfolio, 2010.

Sutherland, Stuart. *Irrationality*. London: Pinter & Martin, 2011.

Tibman, Joseph. *The Murder of Lehman Brothers: An Insider's Look at the Global Meltdown*. New York: Brick Tower Press, 2009.

Vietta, Silvio. *Rationalität: Eine Weltgeschichte*, Munich: Wilhelm Fink Verlag, 2012.

Weber, Max. *Wirtschaft und Gesellschaft: Grundriss der verstehenden Soziologie*. 5th ed. (revised). Tübingen: Mohr Siebeck Verlag, 2002.

Weick, Karl and Kathleen Sutcliffe. *Managing the Unexpected: Assuring High Performance in an Age of Complexity*. San Francisco: Jossey-Bass, 2001.

Woods, David D. et al. *Behind Human Error*. 2d ed. Burlington: Ashgate, 2010.

Zaki, Myret. *UBS: Am Rande des Abgrunds*. Lausanne: Tobler Verlag, 2008.

Zweig, Stefan. *Joseph Fouché: Bildnis eines politischen Menschen*. 48th ed. Frankfurt: Fischer Verlag, 2010.

Zweig, Stefan. *Magellan: Der Mann und seine Tat.* 24th ed. Frankfurt: Fischer Verlag, 2011.

Index

status symbol, 80
Stiglitz, Joseph E., 61
stories, 61, 64, 65, 68, 69, 123, 143
strategy, 19, 22, 24, 28, 57, 60, 65, 66, 67, 87, 99, 127, 128
Strauss-Kahn, Dominique, 94
street fighter, 21, 70, 71, 92
stress, 35, 47, 48, 50, 52, 53, 54, 92, 95, 126, 130, 131, 134, 135, 136, 139
structure, 31, 49, 53, 67, 76, 78, 106, 111, 116, 117, 125, 127, 140, 141, 144, 150, 151
Stürzinger, Walter, 20
subconscious, 51, 53, 54, 55, 56
subprime
  business, 20
  crisis, 35
  lending, 29
  market, 20
  mortgages, 57
success, 11, 13, 16, 19, 23, 30, 31, 32, 33, 34, 40, 53, 56, 57, 63, 64, 65, 68, 70, 71, 75, 77, 79, 80, 81, 82, 83, 84, 86, 87, 88, 91, 92, 94, 97, 101, 102, 103, 104, 105, 108, 109, 114, 115, 116, 117, 123, 125, 128, 132, 133, 137, 139, 140, 141, 144, 145, 150, 153, 154, 155, 156, 157, 158, 159
suffering, 31, 60
superior, 21, 35, 77, 104, 114, 119, 128, 131, 132, 133, 134, 139, 140, 144, 145, 146, 147, 148, 149, 150, 151
Swiss Bank Corporation, 18, 19
synapse, 49
system, 37, 39, 49, 50, 53, 61, 62, 63, 64, 66, 69, 74, 77, 81, 89, 91, 98, 104, 105, 113, 120, 128, 130, 135, 154, 155
  autopoietic, 66
systemic, 13, 37, 39, 61, 66, 128, 130, 155
talent, 42, 50, 67, 103, 108, 116, 119, 150, 156
teacher, 36, 50, 119, 120, 121, 122, 139, 147
team, 15, 21, 29, 30, 33, 42, 44, 50, 60, 62, 68, 69, 79, 82, 85, 86, 87, 91, 108, 109, 118, 134, 136, 138, 143, 146, 150, 158
term limits, 128
Thain, John, 15, 16, 64, 76, 81, 92, 93, 99
thinking
  holistic, 144, 153
  positive, 63, 70, 71, 72, 103
threat, 18, 20, 47, 64, 72, 75, 98, 117, 131, 135, 137, 145, 157
Touche Ross, 27

Acknowledgments

The English version comes eighteen months after the publication of its German original. The translation was possible thanks to Zurich Insurance Group and a few dedicated people, namely Manuel Feierabend, Daniel Neubauer and Paul Mehra who relentlessly looked for the best wording. Thank you!

Zurich and St. Gallen, May 2014
Ulrich F. Zwygart
ulrich.zwygart@gmail.com